C.B. BRODOSKI

Investigation Methods And Tactics

First published by True Nortrhwest Publishing 2024

Copyright © 2024 by C.B. Brodoski

All rights reserved. No part of this publication may be reproduced, stored or transmitted in any form or by any means, electronic, mechanical, photocopying, recording, scanning, or otherwise without written permission from the publisher. It is illegal to copy this book, post it to a website, or distribute it by any other means without permission.

C.B. Brodoski asserts the moral right to be identified as the author of this work.

C.B. Brodoski has no responsibility for the persistence or accuracy of URLs for external or third-party Internet Websites referred to in this publication and does not guarantee that any content on such Websites is, or will remain, accurate or appropriate.

Designations used by companies to distinguish their products are often claimed as trademarks. All brand names and product names used in this book and on its cover are trade names, service marks, trademarks and registered trademarks of their respective owners. The publishers and the book are not associated with any product or vendor mentioned in this book. None of the companies referenced within the book have endorsed the book.

First edition

This book was professionally typeset on Reedsy.
Find out more at reedsy.com

*To the brave men and women of law enforcement and first responders,
This book is dedicated to you—the courageous individuals who stand on the front lines every day, protecting our communities and keeping us safe. Your unwavering commitment, selflessness, and dedication to duty inspire us all.*

Contents

Introduction	1
Introduction	1
Overview of the Book	1
Importance of Understanding Police Procedures	2
Goals and Objectives of the Book	2
Brief History of Modern Investigative Techniques	3
Scope and Limitations	4
Chapter 1	6
Chapter 1: Foundations of Criminal Investigation	6
Historical Background	6
Legal and Ethical Considerations	8
Roles and Responsibilities	10
Chapter 2	13
Chapter 2: Initial Response and Crime Scene Management	13
First Responder Duties	13
Crime Scene Preservation	15
Evidence Identification and Collection	17
Witness Management	19
Chapter 3	22
Chapter 3: Documentation and Reporting	22
Crime Scene Documentation	22
Report Writing	24
Evidence Logs and Inventories	26
Chapter 4	29

- Chapter 4: Interview and Interrogation Techniques — 29
  - Fundamentals of Effective Communication — 29
  - Interviewing Witnesses and Victims — 31
  - Interrogation of Suspects — 33
- Chapter 5 — 36
  - Chapter 5: Forensic Science in Investigations — 36
  - Overview of Forensic Disciplines — 36
  - Crime Scene Forensics — 38
  - Laboratory Procedures and Analysis — 40
- Chapter 6 — 43
  - Chapter 6: Surveillance and Undercover Operations — 43
  - Principles of Surveillance — 43
  - Undercover Operations — 46
  - Use of Informants — 48
- Chapter 7 — 51
  - Chapter 7: Cyber Investigations and Digital Evidence — 51
  - Introduction to Cybercrime — 51
  - Digital Evidence Collection — 53
  - Analysis of Digital Evidence — 55
- Chapter 8 — 58
  - Chapter 8: Special Investigative Techniques — 58
  - Criminal Profiling — 58
  - Behavioral Analysis — 60
  - Geographic Profiling — 62
- Chapter 9 — 64
  - Chapter 9: Investigative Technologies — 64
  - Advancements in Investigative Tools — 64
  - Surveillance Technology — 66
  - Data Analysis and Management — 68
- Chapter 10 — 71
  - Chapter 10: Case Management and Court Preparation — 71

Organizing the Investigation	71
Building a Case for Prosecution	73
Testifying in Court	75
Chapter 11	78
Chapter 11: Investigating Specific Crimes	78
Homicide Investigations	78
Sexual Assault Investigations	80
Property Crime Investigations	82
Drug-Related Investigations	83
Chapter 12	86
Chapter 12: Contemporary Issues and Future Trends	86
Impact of Social Media	86
Community Policing and Public Relations	88
Future of Criminal Investigations	89
Conclusion	92
Conclusion	92
Summary of Key Points	92
Reflections on the Role of Investigators	94
The Future Landscape of Police Investigations	94
Final Thoughts and Recommendations	95

Introduction

Introduction

Overview of the Book

"Investigation Methods and Tactics" is designed to serve as a comprehensive resource for law enforcement professionals, criminal justice students, and anyone interested in the intricate workings of criminal investigations. This book delves into the multifaceted nature of investigative procedures, offering detailed insights into each phase of the investigative process, from the initial response to crime scenes to presenting evidence in court. The chapters are meticulously structured to provide both theoretical knowledge and practical guidance, ensuring that readers can apply the concepts and techniques discussed to real-world scenarios.

The book is divided into twelve chapters, each focusing on a specific aspect of criminal investigation. These chapters cover a wide range of topics, including crime scene management, forensic science, interview and interrogation techniques, digital investigations, and special investigative methods. By exploring these areas in depth, the book aims to equip readers with the necessary skills and knowledge to conduct thorough and effective investigations.

Importance of Understanding Police Procedures

Understanding police procedures is crucial for several reasons. Firstly, it ensures that investigations are conducted within the legal framework, respecting the rights of all parties involved and upholding the principles of justice. This is particularly important in maintaining public trust and confidence in the criminal justice system. Secondly, adhering to established procedures helps to preserve the integrity of evidence, which is vital for securing convictions and preventing wrongful accusations. Thirdly, a thorough understanding of investigative methods enhances the efficiency and effectiveness of law enforcement operations, enabling officers to solve crimes more swiftly and accurately.

Moreover, knowledge of police procedures is essential for collaboration between various stakeholders in the criminal justice system, including law enforcement agencies, forensic experts, legal professionals, and the community. This collaborative approach is critical for addressing the complexities of modern crime and ensuring that justice is served.

Goals and Objectives of the Book

The primary goal of "Investigation Methods and Tactics" is to provide a detailed and practical guide to the principles and practices of criminal investigation. Specific objectives include:

1. **Educating Law Enforcement Professionals**: To enhance the skills and knowledge of current and aspiring investigators, enabling them to conduct thorough and legally sound investigations.
2. **Promoting Best Practices**: To advocate for the adoption of best practices in crime scene management, evidence collection, forensic analysis, and investigative interviewing.

3. **Highlighting Ethical Considerations**: To emphasize the importance of ethical behavior and decision-making in all stages of the investigative process.
4. **Introducing Technological Advances**: To familiarize readers with the latest technological tools and techniques used in modern investigations.
5. **Encouraging Continuous Learning**: To provide resources and references for further study and professional development in the field of criminal investigation.

Brief History of Modern Investigative Techniques

The history of modern investigative techniques is a testament to the evolution of law enforcement and the continuous pursuit of justice. Early methods of investigation were rudimentary, often relying on confessions obtained through coercion or torture. However, as societies developed, so did the need for more sophisticated and ethical approaches to solving crimes.

In the 19th century, the establishment of professional police forces marked a significant milestone in the history of criminal investigation. The creation of the Metropolitan Police Service in London in 1829 by Sir Robert Peel introduced principles of modern policing, emphasizing the importance of preventive measures and systematic investigation.

The late 19th and early 20th centuries saw the advent of forensic science, revolutionizing investigative techniques. The development of fingerprint analysis, pioneered by Sir Francis Galton and Sir Edward Henry, provided a reliable method for identifying individuals. The discovery of DNA profiling in the 1980s by Sir Alec Jeffreys further transformed forensic science, allowing for precise identification based on genetic material.

Advancements in technology have continually shaped the field of criminal investigation. The introduction of computer forensics, digital surveillance tools, and sophisticated data analysis techniques has expanded the capabilities of investigators, enabling them to tackle complex crimes such as cybercrime and terrorism.

Scope and Limitations

The scope of "Investigation Methods and Tactics" is extensive, covering a wide range of topics essential to modern criminal investigations. The book addresses both traditional investigative methods and contemporary techniques, providing a holistic view of the field. It includes discussions on legal and ethical considerations, the role of forensic science, digital investigations, and the use of technology in policing.

However, it is important to acknowledge the limitations of this book. While it strives to be comprehensive, the field of criminal investigation is vast and continually evolving. New methods and technologies are constantly emerging, and legal standards may vary between jurisdictions. Consequently, readers are encouraged to supplement their learning with additional resources and stay updated with the latest developments in the field.

Furthermore, the book is not intended to replace formal training or professional experience. Practical skills in criminal investigation are best developed through hands-on practice and mentorship from experienced professionals. "Investigation Methods and Tactics" should be viewed as a foundational resource, providing the theoretical background and procedural knowledge necessary for effective investigative work.

In conclusion, "Investigation Methods and Tactics" aims to bridge the gap between theory and practice, offering a detailed and practical guide to the art and science of criminal investigation. By understanding and applying the principles discussed in this book, readers can contribute to the pursuit of justice and the enhancement of public safety.

Chapter 1

Chapter 1: Foundations of Criminal Investigation

Historical Background

Evolution of Criminal Investigation
The field of criminal investigation has a rich and complex history that reflects the broader evolution of law enforcement and the justice system. In ancient times, methods of solving crimes were rudimentary and often relied heavily on confessions, which were frequently obtained through torture or coercion. Evidence collection, as we understand it today, was virtually non-existent, and guilt was often determined by public opinion or trial by ordeal.

As societies evolved, so did the need for more systematic and reliable methods of investigation. The development of organized law enforcement can be traced back to early civilizations such as ancient Egypt and Rome, where officials were appointed to maintain order and investigate crimes. However, these early efforts were limited in scope and effectiveness.

The turning point in the evolution of criminal investigation came in the 19th century with the establishment of professional police forces. One of the most significant milestones was the creation of the

Metropolitan Police Service in London in 1829 by Sir Robert Peel. This marked the beginning of modern policing, emphasizing crime prevention and systematic investigation. Peel's principles of policing laid the foundation for contemporary investigative methods, advocating for the use of observation, evidence collection, and community cooperation.

The late 19th and early 20th centuries witnessed the emergence of forensic science as a crucial component of criminal investigation. The introduction of fingerprint analysis by Sir Francis Galton and Sir Edward Henry provided a scientific method for identifying individuals. This was a groundbreaking development, as it allowed investigators to link suspects to crime scenes with a high degree of certainty.

The discovery of DNA profiling in the 1980s by Sir Alec Jeffreys further revolutionized forensic science and criminal investigation. DNA evidence became a powerful tool for identifying suspects and exonerating the innocent, transforming the way crimes were investigated and solved.

Key Milestones in Investigative Practices

Several key milestones have shaped the field of criminal investigation over the years. These include:

1. **Development of Fingerprint Analysis**: Introduced in the late 19th century, fingerprint analysis provided a reliable method for identifying individuals based on unique fingerprint patterns.
2. **Introduction of the Polygraph**: Invented in the early 20th century, the polygraph, or lie detector, became a tool for detecting deception during interrogations.
3. **Advancements in Forensic Science**: The development of various forensic disciplines, such as toxicology, ballistics, and trace evidence analysis, has expanded the capabilities of investigators.
4. **Creation of National Databases**: The establishment of databases like the Combined DNA Index System (CODIS) and the Automated

Fingerprint Identification System (AFIS) has facilitated the identification of suspects and the linking of crimes across jurisdictions.
5. **Integration of Technology**: The advent of digital forensics, surveillance technologies, and data analysis tools has transformed investigative practices, enabling investigators to handle complex crimes such as cybercrime and terrorism.

Legal and Ethical Considerations

Constitutional Rights and Protections

Criminal investigations are governed by a legal framework designed to protect the rights of individuals and ensure the integrity of the justice system. One of the most fundamental aspects of this framework is the protection of constitutional rights. In the United States, the Constitution provides several key protections for individuals involved in criminal investigations, including:

1. **Fourth Amendment**: Protects against unreasonable searches and seizures, requiring law enforcement to obtain a warrant based on probable cause before conducting most searches.
2. **Fifth Amendment**: Protects against self-incrimination and ensures due process of law. This amendment is the basis for Miranda rights, which must be read to suspects during custodial interrogations.
3. **Sixth Amendment**: Guarantees the right to a fair trial, including the right to legal counsel and the right to confront witnesses.
4. **Eighth Amendment**: Protects against cruel and unusual punishment, ensuring that individuals are treated humanely throughout the investigative and judicial process.

Ethical Dilemmas and Professional Standards

Investigators often face ethical dilemmas that require them to balance the pursuit of justice with respect for individuals' rights and the principles of fairness. Professional standards and codes of conduct provide guidance for navigating these challenges. Key ethical considerations include:

1. **Integrity and Honesty**: Investigators must conduct their work with honesty and integrity, avoiding actions that could compromise the investigation or the justice system.
2. **Respect for Rights**: Ensuring that suspects, witnesses, and victims are treated with respect and that their legal rights are upheld throughout the investigative process.
3. **Objectivity**: Maintaining impartiality and avoiding bias or preconceived notions about a case or individual.
4. **Confidentiality**: Protecting the privacy and confidentiality of information obtained during an investigation, particularly sensitive or personal information.

Legal Framework Governing Investigations

The legal framework governing criminal investigations is complex and varies by jurisdiction. It includes statutes, case law, and procedural rules that outline the powers and limitations of law enforcement officers. Key elements of this framework include:

1. **Search and Seizure Laws**: Laws that regulate when and how searches can be conducted and what constitutes lawful seizure of evidence.
2. **Interrogation Laws**: Regulations governing the questioning of suspects, including the requirement to provide Miranda warnings and the admissibility of confessions.
3. **Evidence Laws**: Rules that determine what evidence can be

collected, how it must be handled, and what is admissible in court.
4. **Privacy Laws**: Laws that protect individuals' privacy rights, particularly in the context of digital evidence and surveillance.

Roles and Responsibilities

Law Enforcement Agencies and Their Jurisdictions

Law enforcement agencies operate at various levels, including local, state, and federal, each with its own jurisdiction and scope of authority. Understanding these jurisdictions is crucial for effective collaboration and coordination during investigations. Key agencies include:

1. **Local Police Departments**: Responsible for maintaining law and order within specific municipalities or cities. They handle a wide range of crimes, from minor offenses to serious felonies.
2. **Sheriff's Offices**: Typically operate at the county level and may have responsibilities that include law enforcement, maintaining county jails, and serving legal documents.
3. **State Police and Highway Patrol**: State-level agencies that provide law enforcement services across the entire state, often focusing on highway safety and assisting local agencies with major investigations.
4. **Federal Agencies**: Include entities like the Federal Bureau of Investigation (FBI), Drug Enforcement Administration (DEA), and Bureau of Alcohol, Tobacco, Firearms and Explosives (ATF), which handle crimes that cross state lines or involve federal law.

Investigator's Role Within the Criminal Justice System

Investigators play a critical role within the criminal justice system, working to uncover the truth, identify perpetrators, and ensure that justice is served. Their responsibilities include:

1. **Crime Scene Management**: Securing and managing crime scenes to preserve evidence and ensure a thorough investigation.
2. **Evidence Collection and Analysis**: Gathering physical, biological, and digital evidence, and working with forensic experts to analyze and interpret findings.
3. **Interviewing Witnesses and Suspects**: Conducting interviews and interrogations to gather information, corroborate evidence, and obtain confessions.
4. **Case Management**: Organizing and managing all aspects of an investigation, from initial response to case closure, ensuring that all procedures are followed and documented.
5. **Collaboration with Prosecutors**: Working closely with prosecutors to build a strong case for trial, including preparing evidence and testimony.

Collaboration with Other Entities

Effective criminal investigations often require collaboration with various entities, each bringing specialized expertise and resources. Key collaborators include:

1. **Forensic Experts**: Specialists in fields such as DNA analysis, fingerprinting, toxicology, and digital forensics who assist in analyzing evidence and providing expert testimony.
2. **Legal Professionals**: Prosecutors, defense attorneys, and judges who play critical roles in the legal process, from charging decisions to courtroom proceedings.
3. **Community Partners**: Community organizations, neighborhood watch groups, and citizens who can provide valuable information and support during investigations.
4. **Other Law Enforcement Agencies**: Collaboration with local, state, and federal agencies to share information, resources, and

expertise, particularly in complex or multi-jurisdictional cases.

In conclusion, the foundations of criminal investigation are built on a rich historical background, a robust legal and ethical framework, and the critical roles and responsibilities of law enforcement professionals. By understanding these foundations, investigators can conduct their work with integrity, effectiveness, and a commitment to justice.

Chapter 2

Chapter 2: Initial Response and Crime Scene Management

First Responder Duties

When law enforcement officers arrive at the scene of a crime, their actions during the initial response are critical to the success of the subsequent investigation. First responders have a range of responsibilities that must be executed promptly and effectively to ensure the integrity of the crime scene and the safety of everyone involved.

Securing the Scene

The first priority for any responding officer is to secure the scene to ensure the safety of victims, bystanders, and officers. This involves several key steps:

1. **Assessing the Scene**: Upon arrival, officers must quickly assess the situation to determine if there are any immediate threats. This includes checking for armed suspects, hazardous materials, or unstable structures.
2. **Neutralizing Threats**: If there are any active threats, officers must take appropriate action to neutralize them. This may involve

INVESTIGATION METHODS AND TACTICS

apprehending suspects, providing cover for potential victims, and calling for backup if necessary.

3. **Establishing Control**: Officers need to establish control over the scene by setting up barriers and controlling access points. This prevents unauthorized individuals from entering the crime scene and potentially contaminating evidence.
4. **Setting Up a Command Post**: Establishing a command post allows for better coordination and communication among responding officers and other emergency personnel. It also serves as a centralized location for decision-making and resource allocation.

Providing Medical Assistance

Once the scene is secured, the next priority is to provide medical assistance to any injured individuals. This involves:

1. **Assessing Injuries**: Officers must quickly assess the injuries of victims and provide basic first aid if they are trained to do so.
2. **Requesting Medical Personnel**: Immediate communication with emergency medical services (EMS) is crucial. Officers should provide detailed information about the number of injured individuals and the nature of their injuries.
3. **Preserving Life**: While providing medical assistance, it is essential to avoid disturbing potential evidence. Officers should document the original positions of victims and any medical interventions performed.
4. **Evacuating the Injured**: If the injured need to be moved, officers should ensure that it is done in a manner that minimizes disruption to the crime scene. Any movement should be documented thoroughly.

Establishing a Perimeter

Creating a secure perimeter around the crime scene is vital to preserve evidence and maintain the integrity of the investigation. Key steps include:

1. **Determining the Size of the Perimeter**: The perimeter should be large enough to encompass all potential evidence and allow for a safe working area for investigators. It is often better to overestimate the size initially and reduce it later if necessary.
2. **Using Physical Barriers**: Crime scene tape, barricades, or vehicles can be used to establish physical barriers that clearly delineate the boundaries of the crime scene.
3. **Controlling Access**: Only authorized personnel should be allowed within the perimeter. An access log should be maintained to record the names and times of all individuals entering and exiting the crime scene.
4. **Assigning Perimeter Guards**: Officers should be assigned to guard key access points to prevent unauthorized entry and to provide information to onlookers or the media without compromising the investigation.

Crime Scene Preservation

Preserving the crime scene is crucial to maintaining the integrity of the evidence and ensuring a successful investigation and prosecution.

Importance of Scene Integrity

The integrity of the crime scene must be preserved to ensure that evidence is not contaminated, altered, or destroyed. Maintaining scene integrity involves:

1. **Preventing Contamination**: Uncontrolled entry to the crime scene can introduce contaminants that can compromise evidence.

INVESTIGATION METHODS AND TACTICS

Officers must ensure that all individuals entering the scene follow strict protocols, including wearing protective clothing and limiting physical contact with evidence.

2. **Avoiding Alteration**: It is essential to avoid moving or altering any objects within the crime scene unless absolutely necessary. Any alterations must be documented in detail.
3. **Documenting the Scene**: A thorough documentation process, including notes, photographs, and sketches, helps preserve the scene's original state for further analysis and court presentations.

Methods to Prevent Contamination

To prevent contamination of the crime scene, officers should implement the following practices:

1. **Use of Protective Gear**: All personnel entering the crime scene should wear gloves, shoe covers, and other protective gear to minimize the risk of introducing contaminants.
2. **Establishing Clean Zones**: Creating designated clean zones within the crime scene allows for areas where personnel can don and doff protective gear and equipment without contaminating evidence.
3. **Implementing Evidence Handling Protocols**: Specific protocols for collecting, packaging, and transporting evidence help prevent contamination. This includes using clean tools for each piece of evidence and sealing evidence bags immediately after collection.
4. **Minimizing Movement**: Limiting the number of personnel who enter the crime scene and restricting their movement within the scene helps reduce the risk of contamination.

Documentation Procedures

Proper documentation is essential to preserving the crime scene and creating a reliable record for future analysis and legal proceedings. Key documentation procedures include:

1. **Note-Taking**: Detailed notes should be taken throughout the investigation, including descriptions of the scene, the condition of evidence, and the actions taken by officers. These notes should be clear, concise, and accurate.
2. **Photography**: Comprehensive photographic documentation of the crime scene is crucial. This includes wide-angle shots of the entire scene, medium-range photos of specific areas, and close-ups of individual pieces of evidence. Photographs should be taken before any evidence is moved or collected.
3. **Videography**: In some cases, video recordings can provide a more dynamic and comprehensive view of the crime scene. This can be particularly useful for capturing the layout and context of the scene.
4. **Sketching**: Creating detailed sketches of the crime scene helps provide a visual representation of the location of evidence and the overall scene layout. Sketches should include measurements and be accompanied by a legend explaining key elements.

Evidence Identification and Collection

The identification and collection of evidence are critical steps in the investigative process. Proper techniques and protocols must be followed to ensure that evidence is collected in a manner that preserves its integrity and admissibility in court.

Types of Evidence

Evidence can be classified into various types, each requiring specific collection and preservation techniques:

1. **Physical Evidence**: Tangible items such as weapons, clothing, and tools. This type of evidence is often visible and can provide direct links between the suspect, victim, and crime scene.
2. **Biological Evidence**: Samples that originate from living organisms, such as blood, saliva, hair, and skin cells. Biological evidence can be analyzed for DNA, providing a powerful tool for identification.
3. **Digital Evidence**: Information stored or transmitted in digital form, including emails, text messages, computer files, and metadata. Digital evidence requires specialized techniques for collection and analysis.

Proper Collection Techniques

Collecting evidence properly is essential to maintaining its integrity and ensuring its admissibility in court. Key techniques include:

1. **Using Appropriate Tools**: Different types of evidence require different tools for collection. For example, tweezers and swabs may be used for biological samples, while gloves and forceps are appropriate for physical evidence.
2. **Packaging and Labeling**: Evidence should be placed in appropriate containers to prevent contamination and degradation. Each piece of evidence should be labeled with identifying information, including the date, time, location, and collector's name.
3. **Sealing Evidence**: After collection, evidence should be sealed in tamper-proof packaging to maintain the chain of custody. Any opening and resealing must be documented.
4. **Transporting Evidence**: Evidence must be transported to the laboratory or storage facility in a manner that prevents damage or contamination. This may involve using insulated containers for biological samples or anti-static bags for digital evidence.

Chain of Custody Protocols

Maintaining a clear and unbroken chain of custody is vital to ensuring the admissibility of evidence in court. Chain of custody protocols include:

1. **Documentation**: A detailed record must be kept of everyone who handles the evidence, including dates, times, and actions taken. This documentation helps establish the integrity and continuity of the evidence.
2. **Secure Storage**: Evidence should be stored in secure facilities with controlled access to prevent unauthorized handling. Storage conditions should be appropriate for the type of evidence to prevent degradation.
3. **Transfer Procedures**: When evidence is transferred from one person or facility to another, it must be documented and conducted in a manner that maintains its integrity. This includes using secure containers and transport methods.

Witness Management

Witnesses can provide crucial information that helps piece together the events of a crime. Proper management of witnesses is essential to obtaining reliable and accurate information.

Identifying and Separating Witnesses

Upon arriving at the crime scene, officers should quickly identify and separate witnesses to prevent them from influencing each other's accounts. Steps include:

1. **Identifying Witnesses**: Officers should identify potential witnesses by canvassing the area and asking bystanders if they saw or heard anything related to the crime.

2. **Separating Witnesses**: To avoid contamination of their testimonies, witnesses should be separated and interviewed individually. This helps ensure that their accounts are independent and not influenced by others.
3. **Documenting Witnesses**: The identities and contact information of all witnesses should be recorded, along with a brief description of what they observed.

Initial Witness Interviews

Conducting initial interviews with witnesses at the scene can provide valuable information that guides the investigation. Key steps include:

1. **Establishing Rapport**: Building rapport with witnesses helps them feel comfortable and more willing to share information. This involves being respectful, empathetic, and professional.
2. **Asking Open-Ended Questions**: Open-ended questions encourage witnesses to provide detailed and comprehensive accounts of what they observed. Avoid leading questions that may influence their responses.
3. **Taking Detailed Notes**: Detailed notes should be taken during the interview to capture the witness's statements accurately. These notes will be crucial for follow-up interviews and legal proceedings.
4. **Recording Interviews**: If possible, interviews should be audio or video recorded to ensure an accurate record of the witness's statements.

Maintaining Witness Cooperation

Ensuring ongoing cooperation from witnesses is essential for the duration of the investigation and any subsequent legal proceedings. Strategies include:

1. **Regular Communication**: Keeping witnesses informed about the progress of the investigation helps maintain their interest and cooperation. This includes updating them on significant developments and explaining the importance of their role.
2. **Providing Support**: Witnesses may need support services, such as counseling or protection, especially if they feel threatened or traumatized. Providing these services helps ensure their well-being and willingness to cooperate.
3. **Addressing Concerns**: Witnesses may have concerns about their safety or the potential impact of their testimony. Addressing these concerns promptly and effectively helps build trust and confidence in the investigative process.
4. **Recognizing Contributions**: Acknowledging and appreciating the contributions of witnesses can foster a positive relationship and encourage their continued cooperation.

In conclusion, the initial response and management of the crime scene are foundational elements of a successful criminal investigation. By following established protocols for securing the scene, preserving evidence, collecting information, and managing witnesses, investigators can lay the groundwork for a thorough and effective investigation that upholds the principles of justice and integrity.

Chapter 3

Chapter 3: Documentation and Reporting

Crime Scene Documentation

Effective documentation is the cornerstone of any criminal investigation. It ensures that information is accurately recorded, preserved, and communicated throughout the investigative process. This chapter will explore the various methods and techniques used to document crime scenes, including note-taking, photography, videography, and sketching. Additionally, it will cover the importance of report writing and the maintenance of evidence logs and inventories.

Note-taking and Field Notes

Field notes are the first line of documentation at a crime scene. They provide a real-time record of observations, actions taken, and initial impressions. Proper note-taking involves several key practices:

1. **Clarity and Legibility**: Notes should be clear, concise, and legible. Abbreviations and shorthand can be used for efficiency but must be consistent and understandable.
2. **Chronological Order**: Record events in the order they occur to

provide a clear timeline. Include dates, times, and locations for all entries.
3. **Detail-Oriented**: Include detailed descriptions of the crime scene, the condition of evidence, and the actions of individuals present. Notes should cover who, what, when, where, why, and how.
4. **Objective Language**: Avoid subjective opinions or conclusions. Notes should be factual and based on observations.
5. **Continuous Updates**: Update notes throughout the investigation to ensure that no detail is overlooked.

Photography and Videography Techniques

Photographic and video documentation provide visual records that capture the crime scene's state and help investigators, forensic experts, and the court understand the context and layout.

1. **Overall Views**: Begin with wide-angle shots that capture the entire scene from multiple angles. This establishes the scene's context and shows the relationship between different areas.
2. **Intermediate Views**: Take medium-range photos that focus on specific areas or groups of evidence. These photos should provide a closer look while still maintaining some context.
3. **Close-Up Views**: Capture detailed images of individual pieces of evidence. Use scales (rulers or markers) to show size and ensure clarity.
4. **Sequential Photography**: Follow a logical sequence that moves from the perimeter of the scene to its center, ensuring all areas are documented systematically.
5. **Lighting and Angles**: Adjust lighting to avoid shadows and glare, and use various angles to ensure all details are visible. Consider using flash, reflectors, or alternate light sources when necessary.
6. **Video Documentation**: Video recordings provide a dynamic

view of the scene. Use slow, steady movements to capture the layout and provide narration to describe what is being filmed.

Sketching the Scene

Sketches complement photographs and notes by providing a drawn representation of the crime scene, highlighting spatial relationships and the position of evidence.

1. **Rough Sketches**: Create initial sketches at the scene to capture key details and measurements. These sketches are often rough and may lack precision but are essential for recording initial impressions.
2. **Final Sketches**: Produce detailed, scaled sketches based on the rough sketches and additional measurements. These should include all pertinent details, such as evidence locations, furniture, and fixed structures.
3. **Measurements**: Use measuring tapes, laser rangefinders, or other tools to obtain accurate distances and dimensions. Document these measurements on the sketch.
4. **Legend and Labels**: Include a legend that explains symbols and labels used in the sketch. Each piece of evidence and significant feature should be clearly marked and numbered.
5. **Orientation**: Indicate the orientation (north) on the sketch to provide a reference for directions.

Report Writing

Writing accurate and detailed reports is essential for documenting the findings of an investigation and communicating them to other stakeholders in the criminal justice system.

Importance of Accurate and Detailed Reports

Reports serve as official records of the investigation and can be used in court proceedings, internal reviews, and future investigations. They must be:

1. **Comprehensive**: Cover all aspects of the investigation, including initial response, evidence collection, witness statements, and follow-up actions.
2. **Accurate**: Ensure that all information is correct and verifiable. Errors or inaccuracies can undermine the investigation and its outcomes.
3. **Objective**: Maintain objectivity and avoid personal biases or opinions. Reports should present facts and evidence without drawing conclusions or making assumptions.

Structuring Investigative Reports

A well-structured report helps ensure clarity and coherence. Common sections include:

1. **Introduction**: Provide an overview of the case, including the nature of the crime, date, time, location, and the officers involved.
2. **Summary of Events**: Summarize the key events leading up to and following the crime. Include the initial response, actions taken at the scene, and any significant developments.
3. **Detailed Description of the Scene**: Describe the crime scene in detail, including the condition of the area, the layout, and any notable features.
4. **Evidence Collected**: List all evidence collected, including descriptions, locations, and the methods used for collection. Include photographs and sketches as attachments.
5. **Witness Statements**: Summarize statements from witnesses, including their observations and any relevant information they provided.

6. **Actions Taken**: Document all actions taken by officers and investigators, including interviews, searches, and other investigative activities.
7. **Conclusion**: Provide a brief conclusion that summarizes the findings of the investigation and any recommendations for further action.

Common Pitfalls and Best Practices

Avoiding common pitfalls and following best practices can enhance the quality of investigative reports:

1. **Avoiding Jargon**: Use clear, plain language that is easily understood by non-experts. Avoid jargon or technical terms unless necessary.
2. **Ensuring Consistency**: Use consistent terminology and formatting throughout the report. This helps maintain clarity and professionalism.
3. **Proofreading and Reviewing**: Proofread reports for errors and inconsistencies. Have another officer or supervisor review the report for accuracy and completeness.
4. **Timeliness**: Complete reports promptly to ensure that information is fresh and accurate. Delays can lead to forgotten details and inaccuracies.

Evidence Logs and Inventories

Maintaining detailed evidence logs and inventories is critical to the integrity of the investigation and the admissibility of evidence in court.

Creating and Maintaining Evidence Logs

Evidence logs provide a comprehensive record of all evidence collected during an investigation. Key components include:

1. **Detailed Entries**: Each piece of evidence should have a detailed log entry that includes a description, the date and time of collection, the location where it was found, and the name of the officer who collected it.
2. **Unique Identifiers**: Assign unique identifiers or case numbers to each piece of evidence to ensure it can be easily tracked and referenced.
3. **Regular Updates**: Continuously update the log to include any changes in the status or location of evidence, such as transfers to laboratories or courts.

Proper Labeling and Storage of Evidence

Proper labeling and storage are essential to preserving evidence and maintaining the chain of custody:

1. **Labeling**: Each piece of evidence should be labeled with identifying information, including the case number, description, date and time of collection, and the collector's name. Labels should be durable and securely attached.
2. **Packaging**: Use appropriate packaging materials to protect evidence from contamination and degradation. For example, biological evidence should be stored in breathable containers to prevent mold growth, while digital evidence should be kept in anti-static bags.
3. **Secure Storage**: Store evidence in secure facilities with controlled access. This ensures that only authorized personnel can access the evidence and helps prevent tampering or loss.

Ensuring Accuracy and Accountability

Maintaining the accuracy and accountability of evidence logs and inventories is crucial for the integrity of the investigation:

1. **Chain of Custody Forms**: Use chain of custody forms to document every transfer and handling of evidence. These forms should include the names of individuals involved, dates, times, and reasons for the transfer.
2. **Audits and Reviews**: Conduct regular audits and reviews of evidence logs and storage facilities to ensure compliance with protocols and identify any discrepancies or issues.
3. **Training and Oversight**: Provide training for officers and investigators on proper evidence handling procedures. Implement oversight mechanisms to ensure adherence to best practices.

In conclusion, meticulous documentation and reporting are foundational elements of a successful investigation. By following established protocols for note-taking, photography, sketching, report writing, and evidence management, investigators can create a reliable and comprehensive record of the investigation that supports the pursuit of justice and the integrity of the criminal justice system.

Chapter 4

Chapter 4: Interview and Interrogation Techniques

Fundamentals of Effective Communication

Effective communication is essential in interviews and interrogations. It not only helps in building rapport but also ensures the accuracy and reliability of the information gathered. The success of an investigation often hinges on the ability to communicate effectively with witnesses, victims, and suspects.

Building Rapport with Witnesses and Suspects

Building rapport is the first step in any successful interview or interrogation. Establishing a connection can make witnesses, victims, and suspects more willing to share information.

1. **Establishing Trust**: Trust is the cornerstone of rapport. This involves being honest, consistent, and respectful. Avoid making promises you can't keep and always follow through on your commitments.
2. **Active Listening**: Demonstrating that you are actively listening encourages the interviewee to share more. This involves maintaining eye contact, nodding, and providing verbal affirmations

without interrupting.
3. **Empathy and Understanding**: Showing empathy helps in building a connection. Acknowledge the person's feelings and experiences, and express understanding and compassion.
4. **Professionalism**: Maintain a professional demeanor at all times. This includes being punctual, prepared, and respectful, regardless of the person's status or the nature of the information they provide.

Verbal and Non-Verbal Communication Skills

Both verbal and non-verbal communication play critical roles in interviews and interrogations. Mastering these skills can enhance the effectiveness of your interactions.

1. **Verbal Communication**: Use clear, concise, and simple language. Avoid jargon or technical terms that might confuse the interviewee. Tailor your language to the individual's level of understanding.
2. **Non-Verbal Communication**: Body language, facial expressions, and gestures can convey a lot of information. Maintain open and non-threatening body language. Be aware of your own non-verbal cues and be sensitive to the interviewee's.
3. **Tone and Pace**: The tone and pace of your speech can influence the interviewee's comfort level. Speak calmly and at a moderate pace. Adjust your tone to suit the situation, being firm when necessary but avoiding aggression.
4. **Questioning Techniques**: Use a mix of open-ended and closed-ended questions. Open-ended questions encourage detailed responses, while closed-ended questions can be used to clarify specific points.

CHAPTER 4

Interviewing Witnesses and Victims

Interviewing witnesses and victims requires a different approach compared to suspects. The primary goal is to gather accurate and comprehensive information while ensuring that the interviewee feels safe and respected.

Planning and Preparation

Proper planning and preparation are crucial for a successful interview. This involves understanding the context, background, and objectives of the interview.

1. **Background Research**: Gather as much information as possible about the witness or victim, the incident, and the context. This helps in formulating relevant questions and understanding potential biases or motivations.
2. **Setting Objectives**: Clearly define the objectives of the interview. Determine what specific information you need to gather and what outcomes you aim to achieve.
3. **Choosing the Right Environment**: Conduct the interview in a comfortable and private setting. This helps in putting the interviewee at ease and ensures confidentiality.
4. **Developing a Questioning Strategy**: Plan the sequence and type of questions you will ask. Start with general questions to build rapport and then move to more specific ones.

Techniques for Eliciting Accurate Information

Various techniques can be employed to elicit accurate and detailed information from witnesses and victims.

1. **Cognitive Interviewing**: This technique involves encouraging the interviewee to recreate the context and environment of the

incident. Ask them to recall details from different perspectives and in various sequences.
2. **Open-Ended Questions**: Use open-ended questions to encourage the interviewee to provide detailed responses. For example, "Can you describe what you saw?" rather than "Did you see the suspect?"
3. **Active Listening and Follow-Up Questions**: Listen attentively to the interviewee's responses and ask follow-up questions to clarify and expand on their statements.
4. **Non-Suggestive Techniques**: Avoid leading questions that suggest a particular answer. Allow the interviewee to provide information in their own words.

Handling Traumatized or Reluctant Individuals

Interviewing traumatized or reluctant individuals requires sensitivity, patience, and specialized techniques.

1. **Building a Safe Environment**: Ensure the interviewee feels safe and supported. Use a calm and reassuring tone and provide them with control over the interview process.
2. **Empathy and Patience**: Show empathy and patience. Allow the interviewee to express their feelings and take breaks if needed.
3. **Use of Support Services**: If necessary, involve support services such as counselors or victim advocates. They can provide additional emotional support and help the interviewee feel more comfortable.
4. **Gradual Approach**: Start with general, non-threatening questions and gradually move to more specific and sensitive topics. This helps in building trust and reducing anxiety.

Interrogation of Suspects

Interrogating suspects involves a different set of strategies and considerations. The goal is to obtain truthful information and, if possible, a confession while respecting the suspect's legal rights.

Legal Considerations and Rights Advisements (Miranda Warnings)

Understanding and adhering to legal considerations is critical in interrogations. This ensures that the suspect's rights are protected and that any information obtained is admissible in court.

1. **Miranda Warnings**: Before any custodial interrogation, suspects must be informed of their Miranda rights, including the right to remain silent, the right to an attorney, and the warning that anything they say can be used against them in court.
2. **Voluntariness**: Ensure that the suspect's statements are made voluntarily, without coercion or undue influence. Any form of physical or psychological coercion can render the confession inadmissible.
3. **Recording Interrogations**: Whenever possible, record the entire interrogation process. This provides a clear and objective record of what was said and done, protecting both the investigator and the suspect.

Psychological Tactics and Strategies

Effective interrogations often involve psychological tactics and strategies designed to encourage suspects to provide truthful information.

1. **Building Rapport**: Just as with witnesses and victims, building rapport with the suspect is crucial. This involves showing respect, understanding, and genuine interest in their perspective.
2. **Theme Development**: Develop a theme or narrative that provides

the suspect with a plausible explanation for their actions. This can help them feel more comfortable admitting to the crime.
3. **Minimization and Maximization**: Use minimization techniques to downplay the severity of the crime and its consequences, making it easier for the suspect to confess. Conversely, maximization techniques can involve emphasizing the seriousness of the crime and the strength of the evidence against the suspect.
4. **Presenting Evidence**: Present evidence strategically to confront the suspect with inconsistencies in their story. This can lead to admissions or confessions.

Recognizing and Interpreting Signs of Deception

Recognizing and interpreting signs of deception is a critical skill in interrogations. This involves understanding both verbal and non-verbal cues.

1. **Verbal Cues**: Pay attention to the suspect's speech patterns, inconsistencies, and evasive answers. Signs of deception can include overly detailed or vague responses, changes in tone, and hesitation.
2. **Non-Verbal Cues**: Observe the suspect's body language, such as avoiding eye contact, fidgeting, and facial expressions. While non-verbal cues can indicate deception, they should be interpreted cautiously and in context.
3. **Baseline Behavior**: Establish a baseline of the suspect's normal behavior and compare it to their behavior during critical questions. Significant deviations can indicate deception.
4. **Cluster of Cues**: Look for a cluster of deceptive cues rather than relying on a single sign. Multiple indicators are more reliable than one isolated behavior.

In conclusion, effective interview and interrogation techniques are fundamental to the success of criminal investigations. By mastering the art of communication, understanding the psychology of witnesses and suspects, and adhering to legal and ethical standards, investigators can obtain accurate and reliable information that is crucial for solving crimes and securing justice.

Chapter 5

Chapter 5: Forensic Science in Investigations

Overview of Forensic Disciplines

Forensic science plays a critical role in modern criminal investigations, providing objective and scientifically based evidence that can corroborate witness statements, identify suspects, and exonerate the innocent. This chapter explores the various forensic disciplines, their application in investigations, and their significance in the criminal justice system.

Role of Forensic Science in Criminal Investigations

Forensic science applies scientific methods and principles to the investigation of crimes. It bridges the gap between the physical evidence found at crime scenes and the legal standards required for prosecution. The primary roles of forensic science include:

1. **Evidence Analysis**: Forensic experts analyze physical, biological, and digital evidence to uncover details that are not immediately visible. This can include everything from DNA to trace chemicals.
2. **Linking Suspects to Crimes**: Forensic evidence can link suspects to crime scenes, victims, or weapons. This includes fingerprint

matches, DNA profiling, and ballistic analysis.
3. **Supporting Witness Testimonies**: Scientific evidence can support or refute the statements made by witnesses and victims, providing a more robust case for the prosecution or defense.
4. **Exonerating the Innocent**: Forensic science is also crucial in proving the innocence of suspects. DNA evidence has been instrumental in overturning wrongful convictions.

Major Forensic Fields

Forensic science encompasses a wide range of disciplines, each specializing in different types of evidence and methods of analysis. Some of the major forensic fields include:

1. **DNA Analysis**: DNA profiling involves extracting and analyzing genetic material from biological samples such as blood, saliva, hair, and skin cells. This can identify individuals with a high degree of accuracy.
2. **Fingerprinting**: Fingerprint analysis compares latent prints found at crime scenes with known prints from suspects or databases. Fingerprints are unique to individuals and can provide definitive evidence of presence.
3. **Toxicology**: Forensic toxicology involves analyzing bodily fluids and tissues to detect the presence of drugs, alcohol, poisons, and other substances. This can determine cause of death, impairment, or poisoning.
4. **Ballistics**: Ballistics experts analyze firearms, bullets, and gunshot residues to determine the type of weapon used, the trajectory of bullets, and potentially link a suspect to a shooting.
5. **Trace Evidence Analysis**: This field involves the examination of small, often microscopic evidence such as fibers, hair, glass, and paint. Trace evidence can link a suspect to a crime scene or victim.

6. **Digital Forensics**: Digital forensics involves the recovery and analysis of data from electronic devices such as computers, smartphones, and storage media. This can uncover crucial evidence of criminal activities.

Crime Scene Forensics

The application of forensic science begins at the crime scene. Proper collection, preservation, and analysis of physical evidence are crucial to the integrity of an investigation.

Collection and Analysis of Physical Evidence

The meticulous collection and analysis of physical evidence at a crime scene can make or break a case. Key practices include:

1. **Systematic Search Methods**: Employ systematic search methods, such as grid, spiral, or quadrant searches, to ensure thorough coverage of the crime scene.
2. **Proper Tools and Techniques**: Use appropriate tools and techniques for collecting different types of evidence. For example, tweezers for small items, swabs for biological samples, and vacuum devices for trace evidence.
3. **Documentation**: Document the location and condition of each piece of evidence through notes, photographs, and sketches. This ensures an accurate record and context for later analysis.
4. **Preservation**: Use proper packaging and storage methods to preserve evidence. This includes using breathable containers for biological samples, anti-static bags for digital evidence, and tamper-evident seals.

Trace Evidence and Its Significance

Trace evidence refers to small, often microscopic materials that can transfer between people, objects, and environments during a crime. Despite their size, trace evidence can provide critical links in an investigation.

1. **Types of Trace Evidence**: Common types include hair, fibers, glass fragments, paint chips, soil, and gunshot residues. Each type has specific methods for collection and analysis.
2. **Locard's Exchange Principle**: This principle states that whenever two objects come into contact, there is a transfer of material. Understanding this principle helps investigators look for and interpret trace evidence.
3. **Analysis Techniques**: Techniques such as microscopy, spectroscopy, and chromatography are used to analyze trace evidence. These methods can identify the composition, origin, and possible connections to suspects or crime scenes.

Advanced Forensic Technologies

Advances in technology continue to enhance the capabilities of forensic science. These technologies improve the accuracy, speed, and scope of forensic analysis.

1. **DNA Sequencing**: Next-generation DNA sequencing allows for more detailed and comprehensive analysis of genetic material, improving the ability to identify individuals and uncover familial relationships.
2. **Mass Spectrometry**: This technology is used in toxicology and trace evidence analysis to determine the molecular composition of samples with high precision.
3. **Digital Imaging**: Advanced imaging techniques, such as 3D laser scanning and digital microscopy, provide detailed visualizations of crime scenes and evidence.

4. **Forensic Databases**: Databases such as CODIS (Combined DNA Index System) and AFIS (Automated Fingerprint Identification System) allow for the rapid comparison and identification of DNA profiles and fingerprints.

Laboratory Procedures and Analysis

Once collected, evidence is often sent to a forensic laboratory for detailed analysis. Understanding the procedures and collaboration with forensic experts is essential for investigators.

Process of Evidence Examination in the Lab

Laboratory analysis involves several steps, each critical to ensuring accurate and reliable results.

1. **Chain of Custody**: Maintaining a clear chain of custody is essential from the moment evidence is collected until it is presented in court. This involves documenting every transfer and handling of the evidence.
2. **Initial Examination**: Upon receipt, evidence is logged, photographed, and subjected to an initial examination to determine the appropriate tests and analyses.
3. **Specialized Testing**: Depending on the type of evidence, it may undergo various specialized tests. For example, DNA samples are extracted and amplified, toxicology samples are screened for substances, and trace evidence is examined microscopically.
4. **Quality Control**: Forensic laboratories follow strict quality control protocols to ensure the accuracy and reliability of their analyses. This includes using controls, calibration standards, and peer reviews.

Understanding Lab Reports and Findings

Interpreting lab reports and findings is crucial for investigators to make informed decisions and present evidence effectively in court.

1. **Report Components**: Lab reports typically include an introduction, methods used, results, interpretation of findings, and conclusions. Understanding each section is important for evaluating the evidence.
2. **Technical Language**: Lab reports often contain technical language and scientific terms. Investigators may need to consult with forensic experts to fully understand the implications of the findings.
3. **Evaluating Reliability**: Assess the reliability of the findings by considering factors such as the methods used, the qualifications of the analysts, and the consistency of the results with other evidence.

Collaboration with Forensic Experts

Effective collaboration with forensic experts enhances the quality and impact of forensic evidence in investigations.

1. **Selecting Experts**: Choose forensic experts based on their qualifications, experience, and area of specialization. Ensure they are recognized and respected in their field.
2. **Communication**: Maintain open and ongoing communication with forensic experts throughout the investigation. This includes discussing case details, clarifying questions, and interpreting findings.
3. **Joint Analysis**: Work collaboratively with forensic experts to analyze evidence and develop investigative strategies. Their insights can provide new perspectives and strengthen the case.
4. **Court Testimony**: Forensic experts often testify in court to explain their findings and the methods used. Preparing them

for testimony and understanding their role in the legal process is crucial for presenting a compelling case.

In conclusion, forensic science is an indispensable tool in criminal investigations. By leveraging the expertise and technologies available in various forensic disciplines, investigators can uncover crucial evidence, link suspects to crimes, and support the pursuit of justice with scientifically grounded facts.

Chapter 6

Chapter 6: Surveillance and Undercover Operations

Principles of Surveillance

Surveillance is a critical component of criminal investigations, providing law enforcement with valuable intelligence about suspects, criminal activities, and potential threats. Understanding the principles of surveillance is essential for conducting effective and legally compliant operations.

Objectives and Types of Surveillance

Surveillance operations can serve various objectives, depending on the nature of the investigation and the information sought.

1. **Information Gathering**: Collecting data on suspects' activities, associates, and routines to build a case or inform further investigative steps.
2. **Prevention**: Monitoring potential criminal activities to prevent crimes before they occur.
3. **Apprehension**: Gathering real-time intelligence to facilitate the arrest of suspects during or after committing a crime.
4. **Protection**: Ensuring the safety of witnesses, informants, or

INVESTIGATION METHODS AND TACTICS

potential victims by monitoring potential threats.

There are several types of surveillance, each suited to different situations and objectives:

1. **Physical Surveillance**: Involves direct observation of a person, place, or object. This can be static (stakeout) or mobile (following a suspect).
2. **Technical Surveillance**: Utilizes electronic devices, such as cameras, microphones, GPS trackers, and wiretaps, to monitor activities without the need for physical presence.
3. **Covert Surveillance**: Conducted in a manner that conceals the observer's presence. This is crucial for maintaining the element of surprise and minimizing the risk of detection.
4. **Overt Surveillance**: Performed openly, with the knowledge of the subject. This can act as a deterrent or psychological tool.

Techniques for Covert Observation

Successful covert surveillance requires a combination of skills, techniques, and careful planning to avoid detection and gather reliable intelligence.

1. **Pre-Surveillance Planning**: Thoroughly research the target and the environment. Identify potential risks, escape routes, and legal considerations.
2. **Blending In**: Operatives should dress and act in a manner consistent with their surroundings. This helps avoid attracting attention.
3. **Positioning**: Choose strategic observation points that provide good visibility while minimizing exposure. Use natural cover and concealment whenever possible.

4. **Movement Techniques**: When mobile surveillance is required, operatives should use methods like leapfrogging and parallel tracking to avoid detection. Change vehicles or surveillance points regularly to maintain cover.
5. **Use of Disguises**: Employ disguises to alter appearance and avoid recognition. This can include changes in clothing, hairstyles, and accessories.
6. **Technology Integration**: Utilize surveillance technology such as binoculars, night vision devices, and long-range microphones to enhance observation capabilities.

Use of Technology in Surveillance

Technological advancements have significantly enhanced surveillance capabilities, providing law enforcement with tools to conduct more effective and less intrusive operations.

1. **CCTV Cameras**: Closed-circuit television systems can monitor public spaces, buildings, and private properties. These can be used for both real-time monitoring and post-incident analysis.
2. **GPS Tracking**: Global Positioning System devices can track the movements of vehicles or individuals. This is particularly useful for mobile surveillance and tracking suspects over large areas.
3. **Wiretaps and Bugs**: Electronic listening devices can intercept communications, providing valuable insights into criminal activities. These require strict legal oversight to ensure compliance with privacy laws.
4. **Drones**: Unmanned aerial vehicles offer aerial surveillance capabilities, allowing operatives to monitor large areas or hard-to-reach locations discreetly.
5. **Digital Forensics**: Monitoring digital communications and activities through tools like spyware and network analysis can

uncover criminal conspiracies and evidence of illegal activities.

Undercover Operations

Undercover operations involve law enforcement officers assuming false identities to infiltrate criminal organizations or gather intelligence on illegal activities. These operations are highly risky and require meticulous planning and execution.

Planning and Risk Assessment

Effective undercover operations begin with comprehensive planning and risk assessment to ensure the safety of the operative and the success of the mission.

1. **Objective Definition**: Clearly define the goals of the operation, such as gathering evidence, identifying key players, or disrupting criminal activities.
2. **Intelligence Gathering**: Collect as much information as possible about the target organization, its members, operations, and environment. This helps in formulating a realistic cover story and anticipating potential risks.
3. **Risk Assessment**: Evaluate the potential dangers associated with the operation, including the risk of exposure, physical harm, and legal implications. Develop contingency plans for various scenarios.
4. **Selection of Operatives**: Choose officers with the necessary skills, experience, and psychological resilience to handle the pressures of undercover work. Ensure they are adequately trained and prepared.
5. **Logistics and Resources**: Plan for the logistical needs of the operation, including safe houses, communication methods, financial support, and emergency extraction plans.

CHAPTER 6

Maintaining Cover and Gathering Intelligence

Once an undercover officer is embedded within a target organization, maintaining cover and gathering actionable intelligence become the primary focus.

1. **Creating a Believable Cover**: Develop a comprehensive backstory that aligns with the target environment. Ensure all details, such as personal history, occupation, and lifestyle, are consistent and verifiable.
2. **Building Trust**: Gradually build trust with members of the target organization. This involves demonstrating loyalty, competence, and reliability without arousing suspicion.
3. **Observing and Recording**: Carefully observe activities, conversations, and behaviors. Use discreet recording devices to capture evidence while avoiding detection.
4. **Avoiding Compromise**: Stay vigilant for signs of suspicion or discovery. Avoid taking unnecessary risks and adhere strictly to the established cover story.
5. **Communication**: Maintain secure and discreet communication with the support team. Regular check-ins and status updates are essential for safety and operational oversight.

Legal and Ethical Issues in Undercover Work

Undercover operations raise significant legal and ethical considerations that must be addressed to ensure the integrity of the investigation and the protection of rights.

1. **Entrapment**: Avoid actions that could be construed as entrapment, where an officer induces someone to commit a crime they would not have otherwise committed. This can render the evidence inadmissible in court.

2. **Privacy Concerns**: Respect the privacy rights of individuals not directly involved in criminal activities. Ensure that surveillance and evidence collection are focused and proportional.
3. **Use of Force**: Establish clear guidelines for the use of force during undercover operations. Any use of force must be justified, proportionate, and in compliance with legal standards.
4. **Ethical Conduct**: Uphold high ethical standards throughout the operation. This includes honesty in reporting, respect for human dignity, and adherence to professional codes of conduct.
5. **Legal Compliance**: Ensure all aspects of the operation comply with relevant laws and regulations. This includes obtaining necessary warrants, adhering to surveillance protocols, and respecting constitutional rights.

Use of Informants

Informants, or confidential human sources, play a crucial role in many investigations. They can provide inside information, access to criminal networks, and evidence that would otherwise be difficult to obtain.

Identifying and Recruiting Informants

Successfully identifying and recruiting informants requires careful selection and management to ensure reliability and safety.

1. **Identifying Potential Informants**: Look for individuals with access to valuable information, such as members of criminal organizations, associates, or individuals facing legal issues who may seek leniency.
2. **Assessing Motivations**: Understand the motivations of potential informants. Common motivations include financial gain, leniency in legal matters, revenge, or a genuine desire to help law enforcement.

3. **Establishing Trust**: Build a trusting relationship with the informant. This involves demonstrating reliability, confidentiality, and respect for their safety and well-being.
4. **Recruitment Strategies**: Use appropriate strategies to recruit informants, such as offering incentives, providing protection, or leveraging their legal situation. Ensure all agreements are clearly documented.

Managing and Protecting Informants

Effective management and protection of informants are critical to maintaining their cooperation and ensuring their safety.

1. **Confidentiality**: Maintain strict confidentiality regarding the informant's identity and involvement. Only share information on a need-to-know basis within the investigation team.
2. **Regular Communication**: Keep in regular contact with the informant to provide support, gather updates, and address any concerns. This helps maintain their motivation and reliability.
3. **Safety Measures**: Implement measures to protect the informant's safety, such as relocation, providing personal protection, and creating secure communication channels.
4. **Documentation**: Keep detailed records of all interactions with the informant, including information provided, payments made, and any promises or agreements. This ensures accountability and transparency.

Evaluating Informant Reliability

The reliability of an informant's information is crucial for the success of an investigation. Regular evaluation helps in assessing and managing this reliability.

1. **Cross-Verification**: Cross-verify the informant's information with other sources or evidence to ensure its accuracy and credibility.
2. **Track Record**: Monitor the informant's past performance and reliability. Consistently accurate and useful information enhances their credibility.
3. **Motivations and Biases**: Continually assess the informant's motivations and potential biases. Be aware of how these factors might influence the information they provide.
4. **Risk of Manipulation**: Stay vigilant for signs that the informant may be providing misleading information or attempting to manipulate the investigation for personal gain.

In conclusion, surveillance and undercover operations are essential tools in modern criminal investigations. Mastering these techniques, while adhering to legal and ethical standards, enables investigators to gather critical intelligence, infiltrate criminal networks, and ultimately achieve justice. The effective use of informants further enhances these capabilities, providing inside information and access that can be pivotal in solving complex cases.

Chapter 7

Chapter 7: Cyber Investigations and Digital Evidence

Introduction to Cybercrime

The digital age has brought unprecedented connectivity and convenience, but it has also given rise to new forms of criminal activity. Cybercrime encompasses a wide range of offenses that leverage technology to commit illegal acts, often with far-reaching consequences. This chapter delves into the types of cybercrime, the unique challenges they pose, and the methods used to combat them.

Types of Cybercrime

Cybercrime can be broadly categorized into several types, each with distinct characteristics and targets:

1. **Hacking**: Unauthorized access to computer systems and networks. Hackers may seek to steal sensitive information, disrupt services, or exploit system vulnerabilities for financial gain or ideological reasons.
2. **Fraud**: Includes a variety of schemes such as phishing, online auction fraud, and credit card fraud. Cybercriminals use deceptive practices to trick victims into revealing personal information or

transferring money.
3. **Identity Theft**: The unauthorized acquisition and use of someone's personal information, typically for financial gain. This can involve stealing Social Security numbers, bank account details, or other personal identifiers.
4. **Ransomware**: Malware that encrypts a victim's files or locks them out of their system, demanding a ransom payment for the restoration of access. Ransomware attacks have targeted individuals, businesses, and critical infrastructure.
5. **Cyberstalking and Harassment**: The use of electronic communications to stalk, harass, or intimidate individuals. This can include threats, defamatory statements, or persistent unwanted contact.
6. **Data Breaches**: Unauthorized access to and extraction of sensitive data from organizations. Data breaches can expose personal, financial, and confidential business information.
7. **Cyberterrorism**: The use of digital attacks to cause disruption, fear, or physical damage, often with political or ideological motives. Targets may include government systems, critical infrastructure, and public services.

Challenges in Investigating Cyber Offenses

Investigating cybercrime presents unique challenges that require specialized skills, tools, and strategies:

1. **Anonymity**: Cybercriminals often operate anonymously, using techniques such as proxy servers, encryption, and the dark web to conceal their identities and locations.
2. **Jurisdictional Issues**: Cybercrime frequently crosses national and international boundaries, complicating jurisdictional authority and requiring coordination between multiple law enforcement agencies.

3. **Rapid Evolution**: Technology evolves rapidly, and cybercriminals continuously develop new methods and tools. Investigators must stay current with the latest trends and technologies in cybercrime.
4. **Volume of Data**: Cyber investigations can involve analyzing vast amounts of digital data, including emails, logs, and transaction records. Effective data management and analysis techniques are essential.
5. **Technical Complexity**: Understanding and investigating cyber offenses requires specialized technical knowledge in areas such as computer networks, programming, and encryption.
6. **Legal Considerations**: Navigating the legal landscape of digital evidence, including issues related to privacy, search and seizure, and admissibility in court, is crucial for successful prosecutions.

Digital Evidence Collection

Digital evidence is any information stored or transmitted in digital form that is relevant to an investigation. Proper collection and preservation of digital evidence are critical to maintaining its integrity and admissibility in court.

Identifying and Seizing Digital Devices

The first step in collecting digital evidence is identifying and seizing relevant devices. This includes computers, mobile phones, tablets, external storage devices, and network equipment.

1. **Identifying Digital Evidence**: Recognize potential sources of digital evidence at a crime scene, including not only obvious devices but also less apparent ones like smart home devices and cloud storage accounts.
2. **Seizing Devices**: Secure and seize digital devices in a manner that prevents data loss or alteration. This often involves disconnecting

devices from networks, photographing them in place, and using tamper-evident bags for transport.
3. **Protecting Data**: Use write-blocking devices and other techniques to prevent any changes to the data during seizure and transport. This preserves the integrity of the evidence.

Forensic Imaging and Data Extraction

Forensic imaging involves creating an exact bit-by-bit copy of a digital device's storage, ensuring that the original data remains unaltered during analysis.

1. **Creating Forensic Images**: Use specialized software and hardware tools to create forensic images of digital devices. These images are used for analysis, leaving the original devices untouched.
2. **Data Extraction**: Extract data from forensic images for analysis. This can include recovering deleted files, examining file systems, and analyzing metadata.
3. **Handling Encrypted Data**: Many digital devices and communications are encrypted. Investigators must employ decryption techniques and work with legal authorities to obtain decryption keys when necessary.

Legal Considerations in Digital Evidence

Digital evidence collection is governed by legal frameworks that protect individuals' rights and ensure the evidence's admissibility in court.

1. **Search Warrants**: Obtain appropriate legal authorization, such as search warrants, to seize and search digital devices. Warrants should specify the scope of the search to prevent overreach.
2. **Chain of Custody**: Maintain a clear chain of custody for digital

evidence, documenting every person who handles the evidence and every action taken with it. This ensures the evidence's integrity and admissibility.
3. **Privacy Concerns**: Respect individuals' privacy rights when collecting digital evidence. Ensure that searches are focused and proportional to the investigation's needs.

Analysis of Digital Evidence

Analyzing digital evidence involves using specialized tools and techniques to uncover relevant information and understand its significance in the context of the investigation.

Tools and Software for Digital Forensics

A variety of tools and software are available to assist in the analysis of digital evidence. These tools can automate many aspects of the process and provide advanced capabilities for extracting and interpreting data.

1. **Forensic Suites**: Comprehensive forensic software suites, such as EnCase and FTK (Forensic Toolkit), offer a wide range of tools for imaging, analysis, and reporting. They support multiple file systems and formats.
2. **Data Recovery Tools**: Specialized tools can recover deleted files, reconstruct file systems, and extract data from damaged or partially overwritten storage media.
3. **Network Analysis Tools**: Tools like Wireshark and Network Miner analyze network traffic and logs, helping investigators identify unauthorized access, data exfiltration, and other network-based activities.
4. **Mobile Device Forensics**: Tools such as Cellebrite and Oxygen Forensic Detective are designed for extracting and analyzing data from mobile devices, including call logs, text messages, app data,

and geolocation information.
5. **Malware Analysis Tools**: Tools like IDA Pro and Ghidra are used to analyze malware, understand its functionality, and trace its origin. These tools help identify cyber attackers and their methods.

Interpreting Digital Data

Interpreting digital data requires understanding its context and relevance to the investigation. This involves analyzing various types of data and drawing meaningful conclusions.

1. **Emails and Communications**: Analyze email headers, content, and attachments to uncover communication patterns, identify correspondents, and track message origins.
2. **Metadata**: Metadata provides information about files, such as creation and modification dates, authorship, and access history. This can help establish timelines and identify key individuals.
3. **Log Files**: System and application logs record events and activities on digital devices. Analyzing logs can reveal unauthorized access, system changes, and user actions.
4. **Social Media**: Social media accounts can provide valuable insights into suspects' activities, associations, and communications. Investigators must navigate privacy settings and legal constraints when accessing social media data.
5. **Financial Transactions**: Analyzing digital financial records, such as bank statements, cryptocurrency transactions, and payment app histories, can uncover evidence of fraud, money laundering, and other financial crimes.

Presenting Digital Evidence in Court

Presenting digital evidence in court requires clear and concise communication of its significance and reliability. This involves preparing reports, exhibits, and expert testimony.

1. **Expert Testimony**: Forensic analysts may be called upon to testify as expert witnesses, explaining the methods used to collect and analyze digital evidence and interpreting the findings for the court.
2. **Visual Aids**: Use visual aids, such as charts, diagrams, and screenshots, to help the court understand complex digital evidence. Visual aids can make technical information more accessible to judges and juries.
3. **Clear Reporting**: Prepare detailed yet clear reports that outline the steps taken in the investigation, the tools and methods used, and the conclusions drawn from the evidence. Reports should be understandable to non-technical readers.
4. **Admissibility**: Ensure that all digital evidence presented in court meets legal standards for admissibility. This includes demonstrating the evidence's integrity, relevance, and reliability.

In conclusion, cyber investigations and digital evidence are integral to modern law enforcement. By understanding the types of cybercrime, mastering digital evidence collection and analysis, and effectively presenting findings in court, investigators can navigate the complexities of the digital landscape and bring cybercriminals to justice.

Chapter 8

Chapter 8: Special Investigative Techniques

Criminal Profiling

History and Development of Profiling
Criminal profiling, also known as offender profiling or behavioral profiling, is a technique used to infer the characteristics of an offender based on the details of the crime they committed. The practice has evolved significantly since its inception.

1. **Early Beginnings**: The roots of criminal profiling can be traced back to the late 19th century, with early cases like Jack the Ripper. Although rudimentary, these early efforts involved trying to understand the psychological makeup of the offender.
2. **Modern Development**: The modern era of criminal profiling began in the 1970s with the establishment of the Behavioral Science Unit (BSU) at the FBI. Pioneers such as John Douglas and Robert Ressler conducted extensive interviews with serial killers, which laid the groundwork for systematic profiling techniques.
3. **Advancements in the Field**: Over the decades, profiling has incorporated various psychological theories and methodologies.

The development of computer databases and analytical tools has enhanced the precision and reliability of profiles.

Techniques and Methodologies
Criminal profiling involves a blend of art and science, utilizing both intuitive insights and empirical data.

1. **Crime Scene Analysis**: Profilers analyze the crime scene for clues about the offender's behavior, such as how the crime was committed, the level of planning involved, and any signature elements that might indicate a particular psychological pattern.
2. **Victimology**: Understanding the victim's lifestyle, habits, and behavior can provide insights into why they were targeted, which in turn can reveal information about the offender's motivations and characteristics.
3. **Behavioral Patterns**: Profilers look for patterns in the offender's behavior across multiple crimes, such as modus operandi (MO) and signature behaviors, to identify similarities and differences that might indicate a single perpetrator or multiple offenders.
4. **Psychological Theories**: The application of psychological theories, such as Freud's psychoanalysis or Maslow's hierarchy of needs, helps profilers understand the underlying motivations and psychological state of the offender.

Case Studies and Applications
Real-world cases illustrate the practical applications and effectiveness of criminal profiling.

1. **The Unabomber**: The FBI's profile of the Unabomber, Ted Kaczynski, highlighted characteristics such as his educational background, lifestyle, and psychological traits, which ultimately

helped narrow down the suspect list and led to his capture.
2. **BTK Killer**: Dennis Rader, known as the BTK Killer, was profiled based on his taunting communications with the police and his method of operation. Profiling played a significant role in understanding his need for attention and control, which was crucial in his apprehension.
3. **Green River Killer**: Gary Ridgway's profile included his familiarity with the local area, his ability to blend in, and his methodical approach to selecting and disposing of victims. Profiling helped focus the investigation on individuals who fit this description.

Behavioral Analysis

Understanding Criminal Behavior
Behavioral analysis seeks to understand the psychological and sociological factors that drive criminal behavior.

1. **Psychological Factors**: This includes studying personality disorders, mental illnesses, and other psychological conditions that may contribute to criminal behavior. For example, understanding psychopathy can explain certain traits like lack of empathy and remorse.
2. **Sociological Factors**: These involve examining the influence of social environment, such as family background, education, peer relationships, and socioeconomic status, on an individual's propensity to engage in criminal activity.
3. **Behavioral Patterns**: Analyzing patterns of behavior, such as escalation in violence or consistency in target selection, helps build a comprehensive understanding of the offender's psyche.

Utilizing Psychological Insights

Applying psychological insights to investigations can enhance the understanding of criminal motives and behaviors.

1. **Motivation Analysis**: Identifying whether a crime is motivated by financial gain, sexual gratification, revenge, or other factors helps narrow down potential suspects and predict future actions.
2. **Risk Assessment**: Evaluating the likelihood of an offender reoffending or escalating their behavior is critical for prioritizing resources and protecting potential future victims.
3. **Interview Strategies**: Tailoring interview techniques to the psychological profile of a suspect can increase the chances of obtaining confessions or valuable information. For instance, understanding a suspect's need for control can guide the approach to questioning.

Behavioral Evidence and Its Implications

Behavioral evidence, such as the way a crime is committed or the choices made by the offender, provides critical clues in investigations.

1. **Crime Scene Behavior**: Analyzing the actions taken at the crime scene, such as how the victim was approached, the level of violence used, and any attempts to cover up the crime, offers insights into the offender's state of mind and personality.
2. **Post-Offense Behavior**: Observing how the offender behaves after the crime, including their interactions with others and any changes in their routine, can indicate their level of guilt, fear of capture, or sense of satisfaction.
3. **Linking Cases**: Behavioral evidence can link multiple cases to a single offender by identifying consistent patterns and unique traits across different crime scenes.

Geographic Profiling

Basics of Geographic Profiling

Geographic profiling is a technique used to determine the most probable area of an offender's residence or base of operations based on the locations of their crimes.

1. **Geographic Patterns**: Offenders often operate within a specific geographic area that they are familiar with. Analyzing the locations of crimes can reveal patterns and clusters that point to a central location.
2. **Journey to Crime**: This concept examines how far offenders are willing to travel to commit their crimes. Most offenders commit crimes relatively close to home, with the distance traveled often decreasing as the severity of the crime increases.
3. **Crime Mapping**: Using maps and spatial analysis tools, investigators can visualize the distribution of crimes and identify potential hot spots or areas of interest.

Mapping Crime Patterns

Mapping crime patterns involves plotting the locations of crimes to identify trends and correlations.

1. **Spatial Analysis**: This involves using software to analyze the spatial relationships between crime locations, such as distance, direction, and clustering. Techniques like hot spot analysis and spatial autocorrelation help identify significant patterns.
2. **Temporal Analysis**: Examining the timing of crimes in relation to their locations can reveal patterns in the offender's movements and routines. Temporal patterns can also indicate whether certain times of day or days of the week are more likely for specific crimes.

3. **Environmental Factors**: Considering environmental factors, such as the type of neighborhood, proximity to major roads or public transportation, and land use patterns, helps understand why certain areas are chosen for crimes.

Predictive Modeling in Investigations

Predictive modeling uses statistical techniques and algorithms to forecast future criminal activity based on past data.

1. **Data Integration**: Combining data from multiple sources, including crime reports, demographic information, and environmental factors, creates a comprehensive dataset for analysis.
2. **Algorithm Development**: Developing algorithms that account for various factors, such as offender behavior, geographic patterns, and environmental conditions, helps predict where and when future crimes are likely to occur.
3. **Application in Policing**: Predictive models can inform law enforcement strategies, such as allocating resources to high-risk areas, targeting repeat offenders, and implementing preventive measures. For example, a predictive model might indicate an increased risk of burglaries in a specific neighborhood, prompting increased patrols and community outreach efforts.

In conclusion, special investigative techniques, including criminal profiling, behavioral analysis, and geographic profiling, are essential tools for modern law enforcement. These techniques provide deeper insights into the minds and behaviors of offenders, enhance the understanding of crime patterns, and improve the effectiveness of investigative strategies. By integrating these methods into their investigations, law enforcement agencies can more effectively solve crimes, prevent future offenses, and bring offenders to justice.

Chapter 9

Chapter 9: Investigative Technologies

Advancements in Investigative Tools

Technological advancements have transformed the landscape of criminal investigations, providing law enforcement agencies with sophisticated tools and methods to enhance their capabilities. This chapter explores the significant innovations in forensic technology, their impact on investigative methods, and the integration of these technologies in modern policing.

Innovations in Forensic Technology

Forensic technology has seen remarkable advancements, enabling investigators to gather, analyze, and interpret evidence with unprecedented precision and efficiency.

1. **DNA Analysis**: The development of polymerase chain reaction (PCR) techniques and short tandem repeat (STR) analysis has revolutionized DNA profiling. These methods allow for the identification of individuals with high accuracy, even from minute biological samples. Advances such as touch DNA analysis and mitochondrial DNA sequencing have further expanded the scope

of forensic genetics.

2. **Fingerprint Technology**: Automated Fingerprint Identification Systems (AFIS) have streamlined the process of matching fingerprints from crime scenes with databases. New techniques, such as latent print analysis using alternative light sources and chemical reagents, have improved the detection and visualization of fingerprints on various surfaces.
3. **Ballistics and Firearms Analysis**: Modern ballistics technology, including the Integrated Ballistics Identification System (IBIS), enables the comparison of bullet and cartridge case markings with vast databases. Advances in 3D imaging and virtual microscopy have enhanced the precision of firearms examinations.
4. **Digital Forensics**: The rise of digital crime has led to significant advancements in digital forensics. Tools for recovering deleted files, decrypting data, and analyzing digital footprints have become crucial in investigating cybercrimes. Forensic software suites like EnCase and FTK (Forensic Toolkit) provide comprehensive solutions for examining digital evidence.
5. **Forensic Toxicology**: Innovations in analytical chemistry have improved the detection and quantification of drugs, poisons, and other toxic substances in biological samples. Techniques such as liquid chromatography-mass spectrometry (LC-MS) and gas chromatography-mass spectrometry (GC-MS) offer high sensitivity and specificity.

Impact of Technology on Investigative Methods

The integration of advanced technologies has significantly impacted investigative methods, enhancing both the efficiency and accuracy of criminal investigations.

1. **Improved Evidence Collection**: Technological tools enable more

precise and less invasive evidence collection. For example, portable crime scene scanners and 3D mapping devices create detailed models of crime scenes, preserving the spatial relationships and allowing for virtual reconstructions.

2. **Enhanced Data Analysis**: Big data analytics and machine learning algorithms facilitate the analysis of large volumes of data, uncovering patterns and correlations that might otherwise go unnoticed. This capability is particularly valuable in complex investigations involving multiple data sources.
3. **Increased Collaboration**: Technology has fostered greater collaboration between law enforcement agencies and other stakeholders. Shared databases and interoperable systems enable seamless information exchange, aiding in cross-jurisdictional investigations and the tracking of serial offenders.
4. **Real-Time Decision Making**: The availability of real-time data and advanced analytics tools supports timely decision-making. For instance, predictive policing models analyze crime data to forecast potential hotspots, allowing for proactive deployment of resources.

Surveillance Technology

Surveillance technology plays a crucial role in modern investigations, providing valuable insights and evidence while enhancing situational awareness.

Use of GPS Tracking and Drones

1. **GPS Tracking**: Global Positioning System (GPS) technology is widely used for tracking the movements of suspects, vehicles, and assets. GPS devices can be covertly placed on vehicles or personal items to monitor their location in real-time. This technology is

invaluable in surveillance operations, suspect monitoring, and asset recovery.

2. **Drones**: Unmanned aerial vehicles (UAVs), commonly known as drones, have become essential tools in law enforcement. Drones equipped with high-resolution cameras, thermal imaging, and night vision capabilities provide aerial surveillance, allowing for the monitoring of large areas, tracking suspects, and conducting search and rescue operations. Drones offer a safe and cost-effective alternative to manned aircraft, particularly in challenging environments.

Advanced Audio and Video Equipment

1. **Audio Surveillance**: Advanced audio surveillance equipment, including wireless microphones and parabolic microphones, allows investigators to capture conversations and sounds from a distance. These devices are used in covert operations, undercover investigations, and intelligence gathering.
2. **Video Surveillance**: Modern video surveillance systems, such as high-definition (HD) cameras, body-worn cameras, and covert cameras, provide clear and detailed visual evidence. Facial recognition technology, integrated with surveillance cameras, enhances the identification of suspects in real-time.
3. **Mobile Surveillance Units**: Mobile surveillance units equipped with multiple cameras, audio devices, and communication systems offer flexibility and mobility in surveillance operations. These units can be deployed in various scenarios, from crowd monitoring to stakeouts.

Data Analysis and Management

Effective data analysis and management are critical components of modern investigations, enabling law enforcement agencies to harness the power of information.
Utilizing Big Data and Analytics

1. **Big Data**: The vast amounts of data generated by digital devices, social media, and online activities present both challenges and opportunities for investigators. Big data analytics involves processing and analyzing these large datasets to extract meaningful insights.
2. **Predictive Analytics**: Predictive analytics uses statistical algorithms and machine learning models to forecast future events based on historical data. In law enforcement, predictive models can identify crime hotspots, predict criminal behavior, and allocate resources more effectively.
3. **Social Network Analysis**: Analyzing social networks and communication patterns helps investigators understand the relationships and interactions between individuals. This technique is particularly useful in dismantling criminal organizations and identifying key players.

Case Management Systems

1. **Digital Case Management**: Digital case management systems streamline the organization and tracking of investigations. These systems allow investigators to store, retrieve, and share case-related information, ensuring efficient case handling and reducing administrative burdens.
2. **Evidence Management**: Advanced evidence management sys-

tems provide secure storage and tracking of physical and digital evidence. These systems maintain chain-of-custody records, ensuring the integrity and admissibility of evidence in court.
3. **Collaboration Tools**: Integrated collaboration tools facilitate communication and coordination among investigators, forensic experts, and legal professionals. Shared platforms enable real-time updates, document sharing, and collaborative analysis.

Integration of Technology in Modern Policing

The integration of technology into modern policing has transformed the way law enforcement agencies operate, enhancing their capabilities and effectiveness.

1. **Real-Time Crime Centers**: Real-time crime centers (RTCCs) use advanced technology to monitor and respond to incidents as they occur. These centers integrate data from various sources, such as surveillance cameras, license plate readers, and social media, providing a comprehensive view of ongoing situations.
2. **Body-Worn Cameras**: Body-worn cameras (BWCs) have become standard equipment for many law enforcement officers. BWCs provide a first-person perspective of interactions with the public, promoting transparency, accountability, and evidence collection.
3. **Automated License Plate Readers**: Automated license plate readers (ALPRs) capture and analyze license plate data, identifying stolen vehicles, tracking suspects, and providing valuable intelligence for investigations.
4. **Mobile Technology**: Mobile devices, such as smartphones and tablets, equipped with specialized applications, enable officers to access databases, record evidence, and communicate with colleagues in the field. Mobile technology enhances situational awareness and decision-making.

5. **Cybersecurity**: As law enforcement agencies increasingly rely on digital technologies, cybersecurity becomes paramount. Protecting sensitive data from cyber threats and ensuring the integrity of digital systems are critical to maintaining public trust and operational effectiveness.

In conclusion, advancements in investigative technologies have revolutionized the field of criminal investigations. From forensic innovations to surveillance tools and data analytics, these technologies enhance the capabilities of law enforcement agencies, enabling them to solve crimes more efficiently, prevent future offenses, and uphold justice. By embracing these technological advancements, modern policing can continue to evolve and adapt to the ever-changing landscape of criminal activity.

Chapter 10

Chapter 10: Case Management and Court Preparation

Organizing the Investigation

Effective case management is the backbone of a successful investigation. It ensures that all aspects of the case are systematically organized and prioritized, enabling investigators to build a strong case for prosecution.
Setting Objectives and Priorities

1. **Defining Clear Objectives**: At the outset of an investigation, it is crucial to establish clear objectives. These objectives should be specific, measurable, achievable, relevant, and time-bound (SMART). For example, objectives might include identifying suspects, collecting key evidence, or interviewing critical witnesses.
2. **Prioritizing Tasks**: Once objectives are set, tasks need to be prioritized based on their importance and urgency. High-priority tasks, such as securing the crime scene and collecting time-sensitive evidence, should be addressed immediately. Lower-priority tasks, such as follow-up interviews, can be scheduled accordingly.

3. **Resource Allocation**: Effective resource allocation is essential for managing an investigation. This involves assigning tasks to team members based on their skills and expertise, ensuring that all necessary equipment and materials are available, and managing the budget to cover all investigative activities.
4. **Creating a Timeline**: Developing a detailed timeline helps keep the investigation on track. This timeline should outline key milestones, deadlines for specific tasks, and regular progress reviews. Timelines can be adjusted as needed to accommodate new developments or unforeseen challenges.

Time Management and Resource Allocation

1. **Efficient Use of Time**: Investigators must manage their time effectively to handle multiple tasks and responsibilities. Time management techniques, such as prioritizing tasks, setting deadlines, and avoiding procrastination, are essential. Using tools like calendars, task lists, and project management software can help organize daily activities and track progress.
2. **Delegation**: Delegating tasks to team members based on their expertise and availability is crucial for efficient case management. Effective delegation ensures that no single individual is overwhelmed and that tasks are completed by the most qualified personnel.
3. **Monitoring Progress**: Regularly monitoring the progress of the investigation is vital to ensure that it stays on course. This involves conducting periodic reviews, holding team meetings, and addressing any issues or delays promptly. Keeping detailed records of all activities and findings is essential for tracking progress and making informed decisions.
4. **Adapting to Changes**: Investigations are dynamic and may

require adjustments to plans and strategies. Being flexible and adaptable allows investigators to respond to new evidence, emerging leads, or changing circumstances. This includes reassessing priorities, reallocating resources, and modifying the investigation timeline as needed.

Building a Case for Prosecution

Building a solid case for prosecution involves meticulous preparation and collaboration with prosecutors to ensure that all evidence and witnesses are ready for court.

Collaborating with Prosecutors

1. **Early Involvement**: Involving prosecutors early in the investigation ensures that the case is built with a clear understanding of legal requirements and prosecutorial standards. Prosecutors can provide valuable guidance on evidence collection, witness interviews, and legal considerations.
2. **Regular Communication**: Maintaining regular communication with prosecutors throughout the investigation is essential. This allows for ongoing feedback, clarification of legal issues, and updates on the progress of the case. Regular meetings and status reports help keep everyone informed and aligned.
3. **Joint Strategy Development**: Collaborating with prosecutors to develop a joint strategy for presenting the case in court is crucial. This includes identifying key pieces of evidence, preparing witness testimony, and anticipating potential challenges from the defense.

Preparing Evidence and Witness Lists

1. **Comprehensive Evidence Collection**: Gathering all relevant

evidence is fundamental to building a strong case. This includes physical evidence, digital evidence, witness statements, and expert testimony. Ensuring that all evidence is properly documented, labeled, and stored is critical for maintaining its integrity.

2. **Creating Witness Lists**: Identifying and preparing witnesses who can provide valuable testimony is essential. This includes eyewitnesses, expert witnesses, and any individuals with relevant information. Witness lists should include detailed contact information, summaries of their expected testimony, and any potential credibility issues.
3. **Preparing Witnesses**: Witnesses must be thoroughly prepared for their court appearances. This involves reviewing their statements, rehearsing their testimony, and addressing any concerns or questions they may have. Ensuring that witnesses understand the legal process and their role in the case is crucial for effective testimony.
4. **Evidence Presentation**: Organizing and preparing evidence for presentation in court is a meticulous process. This includes creating exhibits, developing visual aids, and ensuring that all evidence is admissible and properly authenticated. Collaborating with prosecutors to develop a cohesive presentation strategy enhances the impact of the evidence in court.

Anticipating Defense Strategies

1. **Understanding Common Defense Tactics**: Anticipating potential defense strategies helps investigators and prosecutors prepare for counterarguments. Common defense tactics include challenging the credibility of witnesses, questioning the legality of evidence collection, and presenting alternative explanations for the crime.

2. **Strengthening the Case**: Identifying potential weaknesses in the case and addressing them proactively is crucial. This involves gathering additional evidence, corroborating witness statements, and ensuring that all procedures were conducted legally and ethically.
3. **Preparing for Cross-Examination**: Anticipating the defense's cross-examination tactics allows investigators and witnesses to be better prepared. This includes rehearsing responses to likely questions, staying calm under pressure, and maintaining consistency in testimony.

Testifying in Court

Testifying in court is a critical aspect of the investigative process. Effective preparation and communication skills are essential for presenting evidence clearly and convincingly.

Preparation for Court Testimony

1. **Reviewing Case Materials**: Thoroughly reviewing all case materials, including reports, evidence, and witness statements, is essential for effective testimony. Investigators must be familiar with every detail of the case to answer questions accurately and confidently.
2. **Mock Trials and Rehearsals**: Participating in mock trials and rehearsals helps investigators and witnesses practice their testimony and receive feedback on their performance. This preparation builds confidence and ensures that they are ready for the actual court proceedings.
3. **Understanding Legal Procedures**: Familiarizing oneself with courtroom procedures, protocols, and terminology is crucial for effective testimony. Understanding the roles of various

participants, such as judges, attorneys, and jurors, helps navigate the court environment smoothly.

Effective Communication in the Courtroom

1. **Clarity and Precision**: Testifying clearly and precisely is essential for conveying information accurately. Investigators should avoid jargon, use plain language, and provide concise answers. When explaining complex concepts, breaking them down into simpler terms ensures that the jury understands the testimony.
2. **Maintaining Composure**: Staying calm and composed under the pressure of cross-examination is critical. Investigators should remain respectful, avoid becoming defensive, and answer questions truthfully. Maintaining eye contact with the jury and addressing them directly enhances credibility.
3. **Using Visual Aids**: Visual aids, such as charts, diagrams, and photographs, can help illustrate key points and make the testimony more engaging. Properly prepared visual aids should be clear, relevant, and effectively integrated into the testimony.

Handling Cross-Examination

1. **Staying Focused**: During cross-examination, it is important to stay focused on the questions being asked and provide direct answers. Avoiding speculation or over-explaining ensures that responses remain relevant and concise.
2. **Recognizing Defense Tactics**: Understanding common defense tactics, such as attempting to confuse the witness or discredit their testimony, helps investigators respond effectively. Staying calm and composed, and sticking to the facts, minimizes the impact of these tactics.

3. **Correcting Misstatements**: If the defense attorney mischaracterizes the testimony or presents misleading information, it is important to politely correct the record. Providing clarifications and emphasizing the accurate details helps maintain the integrity of the testimony.

In conclusion, effective case management and thorough court preparation are critical components of successful criminal investigations. By organizing the investigation, collaborating with prosecutors, preparing evidence and witnesses, and testifying effectively in court, investigators can build strong cases that withstand legal scrutiny and lead to successful prosecutions. Through meticulous planning, clear communication, and adaptability, law enforcement professionals can uphold justice and ensure the integrity of the investigative process.

Chapter 11

Chapter 11: Investigating Specific Crimes

Investigating specific types of crimes requires specialized knowledge and techniques tailored to the unique characteristics of each offense. This chapter delves into the methodologies and strategies employed in investigating various categories of crimes, including homicide, sexual assault, property crimes, and drug-related offenses.

Homicide Investigations

Homicide investigations are among the most complex and sensitive cases that law enforcement officers encounter. They require meticulous attention to detail, comprehensive understanding of forensic science, and robust investigative strategies.

Initial Response and Scene Management

1. **Securing the Scene**: The initial response to a homicide scene is crucial. The first officers on the scene must secure the area to prevent contamination of evidence. This includes establishing a perimeter, controlling access, and documenting all individuals who enter and exit the scene.

2. **Preserving Evidence**: Preserving the integrity of the crime scene is paramount. Officers must ensure that potential evidence, such as footprints, bloodstains, and weapons, remains undisturbed. This involves careful navigation of the scene and the use of protective gear to avoid contaminating evidence.
3. **Preliminary Assessment**: Conducting a preliminary assessment helps identify the nature of the crime. This involves observing the scene, noting the condition of the victim, and identifying any obvious signs of struggle or weapons. This initial overview guides the direction of the investigation.

Autopsy and Forensic Pathology

1. **Role of the Medical Examiner**: The medical examiner or forensic pathologist plays a critical role in determining the cause and manner of death. The autopsy provides valuable insights into the circumstances surrounding the homicide, including the time of death, the weapon used, and any defensive wounds on the victim.
2. **Collection of Forensic Evidence**: During the autopsy, forensic evidence such as trace evidence, biological samples, and foreign objects (e.g., bullets) are collected. These samples are crucial for further analysis and can provide leads on the perpetrator.
3. **Interpreting Findings**: Investigators work closely with forensic pathologists to interpret autopsy findings. Understanding the injuries and the sequence of events leading to the victim's death helps reconstruct the crime and identify potential suspects.

Investigative Strategies and Case Studies

1. **Witness Interviews**: Identifying and interviewing witnesses is a critical step. This includes canvassing the neighborhood, checking

for surveillance footage, and interviewing anyone who may have seen or heard something relevant to the crime.
2. **Suspect Identification**: Developing a suspect list involves analyzing evidence, reviewing the victim's background, and identifying potential motives. Investigators use various techniques, such as forensic analysis, informants, and public appeals, to identify suspects.
3. **Case Studies**: Reviewing case studies of successful homicide investigations provides valuable insights and lessons learned. Analyzing past cases helps identify effective strategies and common pitfalls, enhancing the investigator's ability to solve complex cases.

Sexual Assault Investigations

Sexual assault investigations require a sensitive and victim-centered approach, combined with rigorous evidence collection and analysis.
Sensitivity in Handling Victims

1. **Victim Support**: Providing support to sexual assault victims is essential. This includes ensuring their physical safety, offering medical and psychological assistance, and connecting them with advocacy services.
2. **Confidentiality and Respect**: Maintaining the confidentiality of the victim's identity and treating them with respect and empathy is crucial. Building trust with the victim encourages cooperation and facilitates the investigation.
3. **Interview Techniques**: Conducting interviews with sexual assault victims requires specialized techniques. Investigators must create a comfortable environment, use open-ended questions, and avoid re-traumatizing the victim.

CHAPTER 11

Medical Examinations and Forensic Evidence

1. **Sexual Assault Forensic Exam (SAFE)**: A SAFE exam is conducted to collect forensic evidence from the victim's body. This includes swabs, clothing, and photographs of injuries. Properly documenting and preserving this evidence is critical for the investigation.
2. **DNA Analysis**: DNA evidence plays a pivotal role in sexual assault cases. Collecting and analyzing DNA samples from the victim, crime scene, and suspect can provide conclusive evidence linking the perpetrator to the crime.
3. **Chain of Custody**: Maintaining a strict chain of custody for all forensic evidence is essential. Ensuring that evidence is properly handled, stored, and documented prevents contamination and supports its admissibility in court.

Profiling and Tracking Perpetrators

1. **Offender Profiling**: Profiling sexual assault offenders involves analyzing patterns of behavior, identifying potential motives, and understanding the psychological aspects of the crime. This helps narrow down suspects and anticipate future actions.
2. **Behavioral Analysis**: Understanding the behavior of sexual assault perpetrators aids in identifying their methods of operation. Analyzing factors such as victim selection, location, and the nature of the assault helps develop investigative leads.
3. **Database Searches**: Utilizing databases such as CODIS (Combined DNA Index System) and ViCAP (Violent Criminal Apprehension Program) helps identify serial offenders and link cases across jurisdictions.

Property Crime Investigations

Property crimes, including burglary, theft, vandalism, and arson, require a thorough approach to identify perpetrators and recover stolen property.

Burglary and Theft

1. **Scene Assessment**: Assessing the crime scene involves identifying points of entry, examining security footage, and collecting physical evidence such as fingerprints, tool marks, and shoe prints.
2. **Stolen Property Tracking**: Tracking stolen property involves checking pawn shops, online marketplaces, and databases for reported stolen items. Investigators work with victims to compile detailed lists of stolen items, including serial numbers and photographs.
3. **Neighborhood Canvassing**: Conducting a neighborhood canvass helps identify potential witnesses and gather additional information. Speaking with neighbors and reviewing any available security footage can provide valuable leads.

Vandalism and Arson

1. **Crime Scene Examination**: Examining the scene of vandalism or arson involves documenting damage, collecting physical evidence, and determining the method of the crime. In arson cases, identifying the point of origin and accelerants used is critical.
2. **Forensic Analysis**: Forensic analysis of evidence, such as paint samples in vandalism cases or fire debris in arson cases, helps identify suspects and establish links to other crimes. Collaboration with forensic experts enhances the investigation.
3. **Community Involvement**: Engaging the community in property

crime investigations is vital. Encouraging residents to report suspicious activities, provide information, and participate in neighborhood watch programs enhances crime prevention and detection efforts.

Drug-Related Investigations

Drug-related investigations involve identifying and dismantling drug networks, conducting undercover operations, and collaborating with various agencies.

Identifying Drug Activity and Networks

1. **Intelligence Gathering**: Gathering intelligence on drug activity involves monitoring known drug locations, using informants, and conducting surveillance. Identifying key players and understanding the structure of drug networks is essential.
2. **Financial Investigations**: Analyzing financial records, such as bank statements and transaction histories, helps identify money laundering activities and trace the flow of drug profits. This often leads to uncovering larger networks and connections.
3. **Community Tips and Complaints**: Encouraging community members to report drug activity provides valuable leads. Anonymous tip lines, online reporting systems, and community outreach programs facilitate the flow of information to law enforcement.

Undercover Operations and Buy-Busts

1. **Planning and Preparation**: Conducting undercover operations and buy-busts requires meticulous planning. This includes selecting undercover officers, developing cover stories, and establishing safety protocols.

2. **Conducting the Operation**: During the operation, undercover officers make controlled purchases of drugs, gather evidence, and identify suspects. Coordination with surveillance teams and backup units ensures the safety and success of the operation.
3. **Evidence Handling**: Properly handling and documenting evidence collected during undercover operations is crucial. This includes recording conversations, photographing seized drugs, and maintaining a strict chain of custody.

Interagency Cooperation

1. **Collaboration with Other Agencies**: Drug-related investigations often involve collaboration with federal, state, and local agencies. Sharing intelligence, resources, and expertise enhances the effectiveness of the investigation.
2. **Task Forces and Joint Operations**: Participating in task forces and joint operations allows for coordinated efforts to target large drug networks. Combining the strengths and resources of multiple agencies increases the chances of success.
3. **International Cooperation**: In cases involving international drug trafficking, cooperating with foreign law enforcement agencies and organizations such as INTERPOL is essential. Exchanging information and coordinating operations on a global scale disrupts cross-border drug networks.

In conclusion, investigating specific crimes requires specialized techniques and a comprehensive understanding of the unique challenges associated with each type of offense. By employing tailored strategies for homicide, sexual assault, property crimes, and drug-related investigations, law enforcement professionals can effectively solve cases, apprehend perpetrators, and bring justice to victims. Through collaboration, meticulous evidence collection, and innovative investigative methods, investigators can navigate the complexities of these crimes and uphold the integrity of the criminal justice system.

Chapter 12

Chapter 12: Contemporary Issues and Future Trends

In the rapidly changing landscape of law enforcement, contemporary issues and future trends play a pivotal role in shaping the methods and tactics of criminal investigations. This chapter explores the impact of social media, the significance of community policing and public relations, and the future of criminal investigations through emerging technologies and methodologies.

Impact of Social Media

Social media has become an integral part of modern society, influencing nearly every aspect of life, including law enforcement and criminal investigations. The ubiquitous nature of social media platforms presents both opportunities and challenges for investigators.

Social Media as an Investigative Tool

1. **Gathering Intelligence**: Social media platforms serve as valuable sources of intelligence. Investigators can monitor public posts, track suspects' online activities, and gather information about criminal networks. Social media analysis tools help in identifying

trends, connections, and potential threats.
2. **Public Appeals and Witness Identification**: Leveraging social media for public appeals can be highly effective. Law enforcement agencies often use platforms like Facebook and Twitter to disseminate information about missing persons, suspects, or ongoing investigations, encouraging the public to provide tips and information.
3. **Undercover Investigations**: Social media also allows for undercover operations in the digital realm. Investigators can create fictitious profiles to infiltrate criminal groups, gather evidence, and identify key players without physical presence.

Challenges Posed by Social Media

1. **Privacy Concerns**: Balancing the need for investigation with individuals' privacy rights is a significant challenge. The use of social media data in investigations raises ethical and legal questions, particularly regarding the boundaries of surveillance and data collection.
2. **Misinformation and Disinformation**: The spread of misinformation and disinformation on social media can complicate investigations. False information can mislead investigators, waste resources, and hinder the pursuit of truth.
3. **Data Overload**: The vast amount of data generated on social media platforms can be overwhelming. Filtering through irrelevant information to find pertinent details requires sophisticated analytical tools and techniques.

Community Policing and Public Relations

Building and maintaining positive relationships with the community is essential for effective law enforcement. Community policing and strong public relations efforts help foster trust, cooperation, and mutual respect between law enforcement agencies and the public.

Importance of Community Involvement

1. **Enhanced Cooperation**: Community involvement enhances cooperation between law enforcement and residents. When the community trusts law enforcement, people are more likely to report crimes, provide valuable information, and participate in crime prevention initiatives.
2. **Crime Prevention**: Engaging the community in crime prevention efforts is crucial. Neighborhood watch programs, community meetings, and educational campaigns empower residents to take an active role in keeping their neighborhoods safe.
3. **Addressing Public Concerns**: Community policing allows law enforcement to address public concerns proactively. By understanding the specific issues and needs of the community, agencies can tailor their strategies to effectively address local problems.

Strategies for Building Public Trust

1. **Transparency and Accountability**: Being transparent about policies, procedures, and actions builds trust. Law enforcement agencies should openly communicate their goals, share success stories, and acknowledge mistakes to maintain credibility.
2. **Community Engagement**: Regular engagement with the community through meetings, events, and social media fosters positive relationships. Officers should be approachable, listen to residents'

concerns, and work collaboratively to find solutions.
3. **Cultural Competence**: Understanding and respecting the diverse cultures within a community is essential. Training officers in cultural competence and sensitivity helps build trust and ensures fair and respectful treatment of all residents.

Future of Criminal Investigations

As technology continues to advance, the future of criminal investigations will be shaped by emerging technologies, new methodologies, and evolving criminal behaviors. Law enforcement agencies must stay ahead of these changes to effectively combat crime.

Emerging Technologies and Methodologies

1. **Forensic Advancements**: Continued advancements in forensic science, such as rapid DNA analysis, improved fingerprinting techniques, and enhanced chemical analysis, will significantly impact investigations. These technologies will allow for quicker and more accurate identification of suspects.
2. **Digital Forensics**: The increasing prevalence of digital devices and online activities necessitates expertise in digital forensics. Investigators must stay updated on the latest tools and techniques for extracting, analyzing, and presenting digital evidence.
3. **Remote Sensing and Imaging**: Technologies like drones, satellite imagery, and advanced surveillance cameras provide new ways to monitor and investigate crime scenes. These tools offer unique perspectives and can cover areas that are difficult to access physically.

Predictive Policing and AI

1. **Predictive Analytics**: Predictive policing uses data analysis to anticipate and prevent crime. By analyzing historical crime data, social patterns, and environmental factors, predictive models can identify potential hotspots and times for criminal activity, allowing for proactive policing.
2. **Artificial Intelligence**: AI and machine learning algorithms can process vast amounts of data quickly and accurately. These technologies can assist in identifying patterns, predicting criminal behavior, and even automating routine tasks, freeing up investigators to focus on complex cases.
3. **Real-Time Crime Centers**: Integrating AI and predictive analytics into real-time crime centers enhances situational awareness. These centers can provide officers with instant access to critical information, enabling faster and more informed decision-making during investigations.

Adapting to Evolving Criminal Behaviors

1. **Cybercrime and Digital Threats**: As cybercrime becomes more sophisticated, investigators must develop expertise in cyber forensics, network security, and digital threat analysis. Understanding the tactics used by cybercriminals and staying updated on the latest cyber threats is crucial.
2. **Transnational Crime**: Globalization has led to an increase in transnational crime, such as human trafficking, drug smuggling, and organized crime. Investigators must collaborate with international agencies, understand global criminal networks, and adapt to the complexities of cross-border investigations.
3. **Changing Social Dynamics**: Social, economic, and political changes influence criminal behavior. Investigators must remain adaptable, recognizing and responding to emerging trends and

shifts in criminal activity. Continuous training and education help law enforcement stay prepared for new challenges.

In conclusion, contemporary issues and future trends in criminal investigations demand a dynamic and forward-thinking approach. The impact of social media, the importance of community policing and public relations, and the integration of emerging technologies are reshaping the landscape of law enforcement. By embracing these changes and staying vigilant against evolving criminal behaviors, investigators can effectively protect communities and uphold justice in an ever-changing world. Through innovation, collaboration, and a commitment to public trust, the future of criminal investigations holds the promise of greater efficiency, accuracy, and community engagement.

Conclusion

Conclusion

In exploring the intricate world of criminal investigations through the lens of "Investigation Methods And Tactics," this book has delved into the essential principles, methodologies, and challenges faced by modern law enforcement professionals. From foundational investigative techniques to cutting-edge technologies and specialized approaches for various crimes, each chapter has provided a comprehensive overview intended to equip investigators with the knowledge and skills necessary to navigate complex cases effectively.

Summary of Key Points

Throughout this book, we have examined:

- **Foundations of Criminal Investigation**: The historical evolution of investigative practices, legal considerations, and the roles and responsibilities of investigators within the criminal justice system.
- **Initial Response and Crime Scene Management**: The critical steps involved in securing crime scenes, preserving evidence, and managing witnesses to ensure the integrity of investigations.

CONCLUSION

- **Documentation and Reporting**: The importance of accurate documentation, effective report writing, and maintaining meticulous records of evidence and inventories.
- **Interview and Interrogation Techniques**: Strategies for effective communication, interviewing witnesses and victims, and conducting legally sound interrogations of suspects.
- **Forensic Science in Investigations**: The role of forensic disciplines in collecting and analyzing physical, biological, and digital evidence, enhancing the investigative process.
- **Surveillance and Undercover Operations**: Techniques for covert surveillance, planning and executing undercover operations, and managing informant relationships.
- **Cyber Investigations and Digital Evidence**: Challenges and methodologies in investigating cybercrimes, collecting and analyzing digital evidence, and presenting findings in court.
- **Special Investigative Techniques**: Criminal profiling, behavioral analysis, and geographic profiling as specialized approaches to understanding and apprehending offenders.
- **Investigative Technologies**: Advancements in forensic tools, surveillance technology, and data analysis that are reshaping investigative methodologies and capabilities.
- **Case Management and Court Preparation**: Strategies for organizing investigations, building prosecutable cases, and effectively testifying in court to secure convictions.
- **Investigating Specific Crimes**: Detailed approaches to homicide investigations, sexual assault investigations, property crime investigations, and drug-related investigations, highlighting the unique challenges and methodologies for each type of offense.
- **Contemporary Issues and Future Trends**: The impact of social media on investigations, the importance of community policing and public relations, and the future landscape of criminal investigations

shaped by emerging technologies, predictive policing, and evolving criminal behaviors.

Reflections on the Role of Investigators

As we conclude this exploration, it is evident that investigators play a pivotal role in the pursuit of justice and the maintenance of public safety. Their dedication, expertise, and commitment to meticulous investigation not only solve crimes but also uphold the rights and protections afforded by the law. Investigators serve as guardians of truth, ensuring that evidence is collected ethically, analyzed rigorously, and presented accurately in pursuit of fair and just outcomes.

The role of investigators extends beyond solving individual cases; it encompasses building trust within communities, fostering cooperation with diverse stakeholders, and adapting to the ever-changing landscape of criminal activities. Investigators are at the forefront of innovation, leveraging new technologies and methodologies to stay ahead of criminals and enhance investigative capabilities.

The Future Landscape of Police Investigations

Looking ahead, the future of police investigations promises to be shaped by continued advancements in technology, data analytics, and interdisciplinary collaboration. Emerging technologies such as artificial intelligence, machine learning, and real-time data analysis will revolutionize how investigations are conducted, offering new tools for predictive policing, digital forensics, and crime prevention strategies.

Moreover, the integration of community policing principles will strengthen partnerships between law enforcement agencies and the communities they serve. Building trust, promoting transparency, and engaging in proactive crime prevention efforts will be essential in addressing contemporary challenges such as cybercrime, transnational crime, and social inequalities impacting crime rates.

Final Thoughts and Recommendations

In closing, "Investigation Methods And Tactics" serves not only as a comprehensive guide for current investigators but also as a resource for aspiring law enforcement professionals seeking to understand the complexities of criminal investigations. As we navigate the complexities of crime and justice, it is imperative to uphold the highest standards of professionalism, ethics, and integrity.

To further enhance investigative practices:

1. **Continuous Training and Education**: Invest in ongoing training programs to keep investigators abreast of new technologies, legal developments, and investigative methodologies.
2. **Interagency Collaboration**: Foster collaboration among law enforcement agencies, forensic experts, legal professionals, and community stakeholders to leverage collective expertise and resources.
3. **Embrace Innovation**: Embrace technological innovations and data-driven approaches to enhance investigative efficiency, accuracy, and transparency.
4. **Community Engagement**: Strengthen relationships with the community through outreach programs, transparency in operations, and responsiveness to community concerns.
5. **Adaptability and Resilience**: Remain adaptable in responding to evolving criminal tactics and societal changes, ensuring that investigative strategies remain effective and relevant.

In conclusion, "Investigation Methods And Tactics" represents a commitment to excellence in law enforcement and a dedication to serving justice with diligence and integrity. By equipping investigators with the knowledge, skills, and ethical framework necessary to navigate complex investigations, we contribute to safer communities and a more just society.

www.ingramcontent.com/pod-product-compliance
Lightning Source LLC
Chambersburg PA
CBHW071835210526
45479CB00001B/152